Thinking+ Living like an Architect

Thinking +
Living like an
Architect

Alex Michaelis and Tim Boyd

CLEARVIEW

CLEARVIEW

First published in the UK in 2016 by Clearview Books
22 Clarendon Gardens, London W9 1AZ
www.clearviewbooks.com

ISBN: 978-1908337-030

Editors: Helen Ridge, Caroline Hutton
Copy editors: Catharine Snow, Melissa Jones
Project co-ordinators: Ben Masterton-Smith, Gabby Sellen
Design: Carl Hodson, Bernard Higton
Production: Simonne Waud

Printed in Italy
Colour reproduction by XY Graphics, London

Contents

"The Smiler (Alex) has worked with me and helped me realise my visions since the first Soho House 20 years ago; through Babington to Berlin and to Soho Farmhouse today. And he is still smiling and we are still friends!"

Nick Jones
June 2015

Alex Michaelis ARB RIBA
Partner

Alex Michaelis and Tim Boyd set up Michaelis Boyd Associates in Notting Hill, London, in 1995.

Born in Paris, Alex studied architecture at the Architectural Association and Oxford Polytechnic. He joined Solar Energy Developments in London and Gilles Bouchez et Associes in Paris before meeting Tim Boyd at John Miller and Partners where he was working on a new faculty building for the Royal College of Art.

Alex's projects include the unique residential development of Battersea Power Station, commercial projects for the Soho House Group, among them Soho House Berlin and Pizza East in London. Alex was instrumental in developing Soho Farmhouse in the beautiful Oxford countryside with 30 new build cabins and the restoration of listed farmhouse structures. He also works internationally on projects such as high-end retreats in Kenya and Botswana, the Williamsburg Hotel in New York, a residential project in South Africa, and Pizza Marzano in Shanghai as well as a new build house overlooking the Dead Sea and Jerusalem in Jordan.

Alex is a champion of sustainable architecture, having worked with Solar Energy Developments and, with his father Dominic Michaelis, been a founding member of the Energy Island Group. A chartered member of the RIBA, he has lectured on green design in the UK and internationally, including at the Green Aruba conference 2012.

Future projects include designing his third new build family home in West London on the site of an old MOT Centre, another opportunity to apply innovation and creativity to a challenging site.

Tim Boyd MA RCA
Partner

Tim was born in London, studied architecture at the Royal College of Art and worked at a number of architecture and design practices including the Conran Design Croup, John Miller and Partners, and Richard Rogers and Partners, until setting up Michaelis Boyd Associates with Alex in 1995.

Tim's projects include Michaelis Boyd's commission to design 254 luxury apartments at Battersea Power Station, featuring more than 100 different apartment types intended to highlight the original features that make up this iconic London building. Other significant projects include a new build residential project in Notting Hill, international restaurants for acclaimed chef Tom Aikens, new hotels in Paris and Amsterdam, a new build residential tower in central London, as well as a £12m new build complex in central London.

Tim has both commercial and residential experience and particular expertise with listed, period and character properties for private residential clients, including architecturally important buildings such as Kingham House in Oxfordshire and Elm Park Road in London.

Tim and Alex have led a politically sensitive scheme to design a residential home for Gurkha pensioners living in isolated communities in Nepal. The project presented a unique opportunity to donate time and expertise to help Gurkhas live their lives with pride and dignity.

Both Tim and Alex have a personal interest in furniture design and manufacture, and this has led to Michaelis Boyd developing a bespoke approach to furniture design and selection for clients. In 2012 Michaelis Boyd launched the studio's first furniture collection at Milan's Salone.

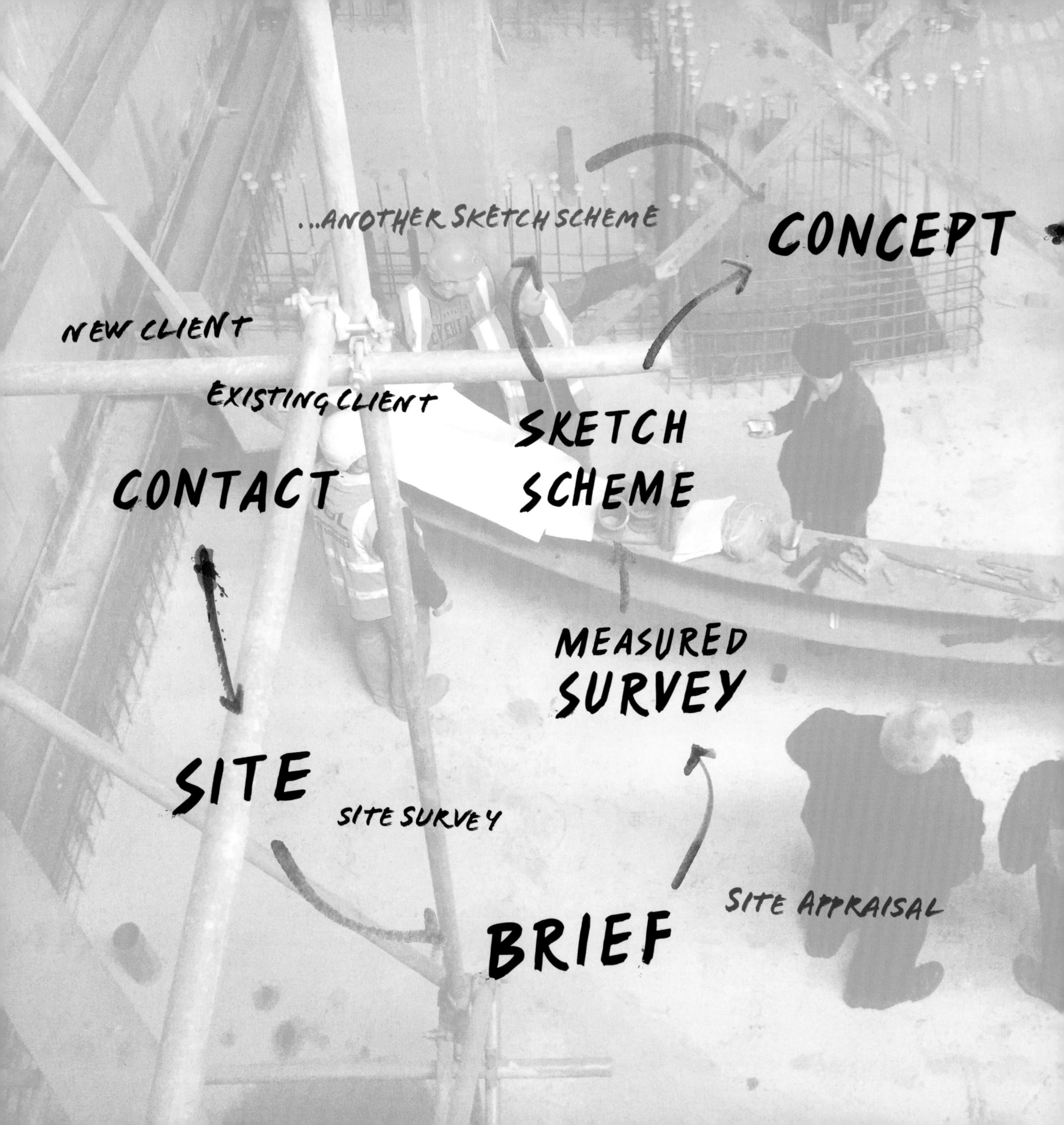

...ANOTHER SKETCH SCHEME

CONCEPT

NEW CLIENT

EXISTING CLIENT

SKETCH SCHEME

CONTACT

MEASURED SURVEY

SITE

SITE SURVEY

SITE APPRAISAL

BRIEF

QUANTITY SURVEYOR

SERVICES ENGINEER

LANDSCAPE DESIGNER

AUDIO / VISUAL CONSULTANT

INTERIOR DESIGNER

PLANNING

DETAIL DESIGN

SAMPLES

PLANNING CONSULTANT

STRUCTURAL ENGINEER

TENDER NEGOTIATIONS

TENDER

COST SAVINGS

BUILD

SNAGGING

COMPLETION

SITE MEETINGS

PHOTOGRAPHY

PUBLISH PROJECT

Chapter 1
Houses in the City

Oxford Gardens
London W10

Architect **Michaelis Boyd**
Landscape Design **Ross Palmer Gardens**

THE BRIEF: To create a five-bedroomed family house of approximately 3,000 sq ft over two floors for the Michaelis family, providing a light and spacious living environment, children's climbing area and an indoor swimming pool. The house would be energy efficient, trialling as many new systems as possible to present to future clients. Yet the site was only granted planning permission for a build no higher than the 5 ft garden wall, as the council wanted to preserve the open space between two other large houses. So this meant that the house would have to be invisible from the street.

As architects we could see the possibilities of creating a unique house in an unusual space – and welcomed the opportunity of showing what could be done below ground without compromising the light and elegance of our approach. While open spaces between buildings are important because they provide light to the streets, this site, in a residential street in North Kensington, was inhabited by foxes, and had become a dumping ground for washing machines, mattresses and general junk. Above ground we had the opportunity both to give the neighbours a more beautiful view and to enrich the eco system with a green roof.

We planted the roof with its own eco-garden, and asked Ross Palmer Gardens to install the sedum and grass roof. Green roofs are common in Germany and Scandinavia and increasingly popular in the UK as people appreciate their benefits, but this was a first for the residents of Oxford Gardens. The roof absorbs CO2 in the atmosphere, acts as insulation and reduces flooding by soaking up rain. People continually peer over the wall, and the house generated a great deal of press, not only because it is below ground but because of the many innovative environmental elements it incorporates.

Left The slide running beside the stairs was a fun means for the children to get down to the basement. The stairs have no risers as they block the light, while the stairwell itself was made as wide as possible to encourage the downward flow of light.

"The planning office said 'you will never build anything here.'"

"The foxes loved the green roof, and used the rooflight as a skating rink."

The main challenge of the project was to ensure that a below ground house would not be dark. In the main room we harnessed day light through an aperture in the roof measuring 2m x 4m, used high level windows to east and west and glazed the entire south façade down to basement level, so that light dropped down through the whole house.

Right – Energy Model: This section shows our plan for sustainable energy throughout the build. The water supply comes directly from a borehole we sank to 240ft, tapping directly into an aquifer fed by water from the Chilterns. Before digging, we checked carefully for plague-pits, of which there are many in London. Once extracted, the water is treated, using a sediment filter and ultraviolet light to kill bacteria.

Underfloor heating was installed throughout, with hot water generated from a heat exchanger - an energy-efficient machine that works using the reverse process to that of a fridge. Solar panels contributed to the house's electricity supply which, when permission for off-street parking was granted, was also used to charge an electric car. The vehicle is exempt from the congestion charge, residents' parking fees and road tax.

We wanted to make the house as environmentally friendly as possible, especially with a swimming pool to heat. We made use of the pool's heat by double glazing and insulating the external walls and single glazing the screen to the stairwell so that warmth could be passed through the glazing into the house. This reduces the need to switch on the underfloor heating and also acts as a heat sync by taking redundant heat from the heat pump it can be recycled to to supplement the pool heating.

Bottom right – Basement under construction: The garden wall had to be retained, therefore we dug out 1,000 cubic metres of London clay in order to clear the way for a deep basement with space for five bedrooms. The owners of the adjoining properties were understandably nervous that their homes might disappear into the resulting hole. To guard against this, the site was underpinned, using 50ft piles that were first filled with concrete and then joined with ring-beams to form a rigid palisade. The project, which affected 36 different owners, required great diplomacy.

Opposite – Living Area: The house is entered at ground level; we created a lateral living space with honed grey limestone floors. Cooking, eating and sitting were arranged in open-plan around the central stairwell, with glass doors leading out onto a stone terrace, big enough for barbecues. This outside space is crucial to the use and open feel of the house.

Clarendon Road
London W11

Architect **Michaelis Boyd**

THE BRIEF: The owners are live-in developers, buying properties, and project managing the build themselves while the reconstruction process goes on. They bought a very rundown 1960s brick house, which had been wedged into a Second World War bombsite, and planned to knock it down to build a bold, modernist house from scratch. Once we had handed over our plans, they were off.

The brief presented us with a problem because the planning department wanted a house in keeping with the rest of the street; Clarendon Road is made up of predominantly Victorian Stucco houses. After careful negotiation we persuaded the council that it would be impossible to replicate a Victorian house in such a narrow space but that a dramatic modern house would be a great improvement on the previous 60s build.

Left: The elevation is an exercise in Bauhaus like minimalism. The plain windows break up a simple white rendered facade. The long slot window above the front door reflects the stairwell behind.

Opposite: The Z stair on the ground floor hides the continuation of the staircase down to the basement. Most developers want to create a house with wide market appeal for an easy sale but the owners did not want to cut any corners and all the detailing had to reflect this. They were not afraid to keep the lines crisp, clean and completely modern. The property sold for well over the asking price.

"Many of our projects are defined by their staircases."

Opposite, top: The open plan kitchen and dining room was situated at basement level, and included a fitted stone floor and sliding French windows directly onto the garden. The idea to create the seamless 'inside/outside' experience was a relatively new concept to the area, and one that we exploited to the full on subsequent projects.

Opposite, bottom left: Another innovation, which became one of our trademarks was the walk-through shower, with enormous showerheads that delivered a 'rainforest' of water. It was this shower and concept that Nick Jones spotted and earmarked for future use in his hotels.

Opposite, bottom right: One of the four bedrooms with views over leafy gardens to the back of the house. As we were replacing a 1960s house with a new-build, there was no need to add in any original features, and the effect is highly contemporary and calm.

Above: The top floor landing is illuminated by rooflights over the stair void, and the glass back to the stairwell allows light to flood downwards. Oak flooring throughout the house warms the cooler white palette of the walls.

Right: Many of our projects are defined by their staircases; it is an opportunity to combine a strong visual design impact with a thoughtful use of space. Space was tight for this project so the stairs run like a ribbon in a void from floor to floor, only turning once at ground level and eliminating the extra space a landing would take up.

"With Pinto, mad ideas became real."

Manresa Road
London SW3

Architect **Michaelis Boyd**
Interior Design **Alberto Pinto**

THE BRIEF: Italian businessman Flavio Briatore had bought this empty shell of a triplex apartment in a historic 19th century Victorian building. It was one of the Candy Brothers' earliest luxury developments, unique in that all the apartments were lateral – constructed over one floor – an extremely rare thing in London. This was the only triplex built and was over 10,000 sq feet.

We were instructed to work with Flavio's favourite interior design company Alberto Pinto Design. They were entertaining in their approach, as the legacy left by its eponymous founder was for large challenging spaces, and this was one of the most enjoyable projects we'd ever worked on.

Left: The elliptical staircase has a curved glass balustrade and is an unbelievable piece of engineering rising through all three floors.

Opposite: Artificial plants create a stunning backdrop in the guest loo – a classic quirky and humorous Pinto touch.

"The Pinto team were very entertaining to work with and mixed confidently simple strong interior design with tongue in cheek statements."

Flavio's friend and business colleague Bernie Ecclestone had bought the penthouse apartment above. While Bernie was content to have low ceilings, we were asked to try and make Flavio's as high as possible. The triplex has five bedrooms,with the rest of the space given over to staff quarters, a spa, hairdressing salon, flotation tank room and two private massage rooms.

Opposite: To counterbalance what was a rather square concrete framed interior, Pinto Design created a vaulted ceiling in the living room which doubles up as a dining room: to the left is a small kitchen where meals can be brought in from the main kitchen.

Right – kitchen: Greater detail of the small kitchen. The joinery is by Kaizen, one of the finest bespoke joiners and furniture designers in the business, whose entire output is made in the UK. The pendant lighting is by Tom Dixon.

Right – bathroom: Kaizen created a 'His and Hers' dressing room with mirrors trimmed in Majilite (a square patterned material), and 'His and Hers' bathrooms, finished off with vanity units with feature mirrors.

Chiswick Lane
London W4

Architect **Michaelis Boyd**

THE BRIEF: Our clients Amy and Marcus Barclay had acquired a plot of land that was surrounded on three sides by the back rows of terraced houses, meaning it was landlocked except for one small point of access. A developer had obtained planning permission to build two houses on this one plot, but only as high as the party wall fences at 8 ft (similar to our work at Oxford Gardens). Just as the first stage, in which the land was excavated to create a concrete-lined hole, was complete, the developer went into liquidation. The Barclays brought us in and asked us to design a scheme with five bedrooms and a strong environmental bias while they were still negotiating to buy the property.

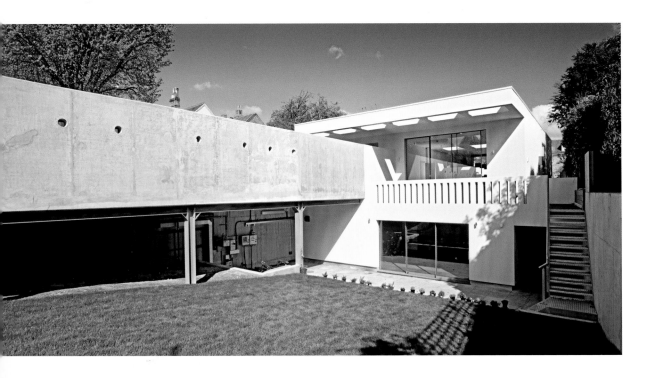

Left: The garden is big enough to fit a tennis court, and here you see part of it with steps leading up to the double height kitchen and dining room. Below is an insulated drum room, with sliding doors onto the garden.

Opposite: A view from the kitchen balcony, showing greater detail of the connecting walkway between the living and sleeping areas.

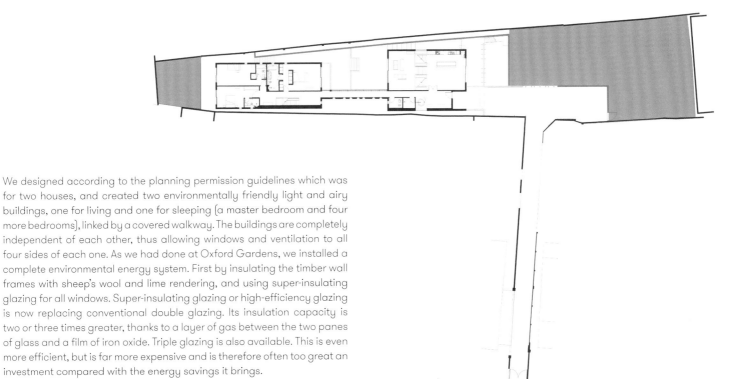

We designed according to the planning permission guidelines which was for two houses, and created two environmentally friendly light and airy buildings, one for living and one for sleeping (a master bedroom and four more bedrooms), linked by a covered walkway. The buildings are completely independent of each other, thus allowing windows and ventilation to all four sides of each one. As we had done at Oxford Gardens, we installed a complete environmental energy system. First by insulating the timber wall frames with sheep's wool and lime rendering, and using super-insulating glazing for all windows. Super-insulating glazing or high-efficiency glazing is now replacing conventional double glazing. Its insulation capacity is two or three times greater, thanks to a layer of gas between the two panes of glass and a film of iron oxide. Triple glazing is also available. This is even more efficient, but is far more expensive and is therefore often too great an investment compared with the energy savings it brings.

Then we installed the heat recovery system. Higher levels of insulation and air tightness in residential dwellings and commercial buildings can cause weak airflows. The resulting poor indoor climate can lead to health problems for occupants and visitors alike and long term damaging effects to the fabric of a building. So a good heat recovery system pulls in fresh air from outside, warms it and delivers it into the house, at the same time as extracting and expelling stale air outside.

Both rainwater and wastewater harvesting systems were installed along with solar panels and a low maintenance sedum roof. Sedum roofs are extraordinary, providing a natural habitat for insects and plants; they also reduce the surface run-off for rainwater, provide further roof insulation and improve the quality of the rainwater itself, particularly if it is being recycled as in this case.

We brought the project in at under £200 per square foot which, given the eco-systems and the complexities of the site we felt was a good result.

Opposite, top and bottom: Starting to erect the prefabricated timber frames within the concrete covered basement left by the previous developer.

Opposite, centre: A view of the connecting walkway between the two buildings, under which is a courtyard with a whirlpool Jacuzzi and sliding French doors into a soundproofed drum room.

Above: The architectural drawing showing the plan for the complete development.

Right: A view of the double height, Bulthaup designed kitchen/dining room, with steps up to an open plan living room. Two flights of stairs take you down to a study, homework room and previously mentioned drum room.

Campden Hill Road
London W8

Architect **Michaelis Boyd**
Interior Design **Honor Riley**
Landscape Design **Philip Nixon**

THE BRIEF: Christopher Bodker, west London developer and restaurateur, who created such restaurants as the Avenue in St James's before turning his hand to development discovered this site - previously a small 1950s two storey house - and saw the opportunity to create two spectacular semi-detached villas.

Left: Our approach was based on understanding the richness of detail on the Phillimore Estate and producing houses that added to the quality of the estate as a whole. Hyde House and Holland House – as each semi-detached villa became known – are faithful to the area's heritage on the outside, whilst incorporating the highest standards of modern construction and minimal energy use inside.

Opposite: Philip Nixon Design, whose work has won three gold and one silver gilt medals at the RHS Chelsea Flower Show, created both gardens to be relaxed, simple lifestyle spaces working in balance and sympathy with the interiors of the houses. The planting was a mix of clipped structural elements and wilder, free flowing specimens. The design also incorporated the clean and elegant lines required for exterior entertaining, dining or relaxing, with a coherent flow between outside and inside.

"Quite simply, these are remarkable houses
that offer a unique living experience."

Our aim was to create two beautiful houses that met the demands of modern living. We brought in space, light and flexibility with rooms that blended into one another seamlessly, allowing families to live as just that – families. The interior architecture had to remain more traditional than we had originally thought; we collaborated with the interior designer Honor Riley on both concept and interior architecture, sourcing materials that were sympathetic to the history of the Phillimore Estate, whilst lifting it into the 21st century. We were able to introduce really up to date finishes, including Crittall glazing, oak, unlacquered brass, and bronze ironmongery, all of which improve with age.

Through this choice of materials and how they have been used, these houses will look as good in a decade as they do today. Here the ultra-modern fuses with the traditional: cutting-edge, user-friendly Sonos multi-room hifi and Lutron lighting systems sit alongside oak floors, brass bathroom fittings, Moroccan tiles in the guest and children's bathrooms and superbly book-matched marble in the master bathroom. We used ground source heat pumps that harness the natural heat from underground to provide warmth in winter and cooling in summer. All at virtually no cost to the owner or the environment, whilst also highlighting our own commitment to neutralizing the carbon footprint of the house.

Above: The core of what you do to a house is how you handle the staircase in order to get as much natural light into the rooms. Here it was the statement piece throughout the house, made of blackened steel balusters and a beautiful timber handrail.

Right: We sourced this kitchen from Bulthaup, their B3 model with a Carrera marble island and Miele appliances. We're often asked why we choose Bulthaup and the reason is not only their design but that they're wonderful to work with.

Far right: The master bathroom shows the book-matched marble, reflected in the mirror which creates a greater sense of space.

Overleaf: Each house has the same 12m swimming pool in the basement. As the original 1950s structure had been demolished the construction of the basement was simplified by having an open site with no immediate neighbours to disturb. Light streams in from the glass skylight to the courtyard. Sustainable hardwood is used for the panelling to the shower and both a sauna/hammam and poolside bar were installed to provide the ultimate in poolside luxury.

Archer Street
Soho, London W1

Architect **Michaelis Boyd**
Furniture Design **Enrico Marone Cinzano**

THE BRIEF: As most of the south side of Archer Street is largely taken up with the backs of the Apollo, Lyric and Windmill theatres, it has become a networking hub for musicians from Soho's music halls, theatres and clubs. The foundations of British rock were laid in Archer Street, where the Shadows, Ray Davies and John Paul Jones of Led Zeppelin played their first gigs. So it was no surprise to discover the apartment we were asked to convert had a musical history and had been part of the Orchestral Association building, built in 1912 and Georgian in style. Today its ground floor houses Boca di Lupo, a smart Italian restaurant.

An internationally acclaimed Italian furniture designer bought the top floor apartment of the building, and his brief was that our architectural and interior plans were to reflect those of his highly sculptural and angular designs. Added to this, he wanted to use only local and sustainable materials in sympathy with our own ideals. The vision was to strip back the apartment to expose the basic fabric of the building in line with the honesty and aesthetic of his furniture. Raw brick, exposed timber and many reclaimed materials were used to minimise the carbon footprint of the refurbishment.

Left: Rock & Roll has left little legacy here, except for an old Casino sign and perhaps the crowds that pour into Soho at the weekend.

Right: The apartment is essentially one long open plan room, incorporating sitting, dining and kitchen areas, with a double bedroom and bathroom leading off it. We designed the flat and all the details working closely with the client on every single fixture and fitting.

"Honesty in design was the only policy."

We were immediately struck by the wonderful light that floods the entire space because of its elevated fourth floor position and westerly light. We installed as many rooflights as possible and remodelled the windows to maximise the views and light. The entertaining spaces are very generous and to enlarge them further we created a small walk through kitchen area.

Opposite: The owner loves to cook so we installed a cooker range over which chopping boards are fitted for when the hobs are not in use. This is a wonderful space-saving device.

Right: The owner wanted the cupboards designed in line with the furniture concept. We designed the faceted doors to reflect the angular design of his furniture. The wood is reclaimed, and sourced no further than 100 miles from London, as was every other feature. We put cupboards in the dining area, kitchen and bedroom resulting in a huge amount of storage space.

Below: This image conveys the contrast between the steel fixtures and fittings and the warmth of the brickwork.

Brackenbury House
London W6

Architect **Michaelis Boyd**
Interior Design **Sarah Delaney**
Contractors **Stella Rossa Ltd**

THE BRIEF: Tanya Roussel had seen this run-down, poorly constructed live-work unit and was struck by the potential to transform it into a five bedroom home. An intimate external courtyard provided a private outlook whilst allowing light to flood into the building. The challenge again was to create lateral spaces by extending and reconfiguring this two storey building.

We designed the ground floor level with full height external and internal pocket doors to enable the living spaces either to be compartmentalised or opened out into the courtyard whenever required. We designed an extension for the kitchen and dining room that overlooked the back garden, and planted a rooftop terrace above it, to compensate for the garden space we had stolen.

Opposite: The garden was completely relandscaped to create a green, peaceful space all year round.

Above: Once inside the front door, the whole ground floor stretches out in front of you like an enormous loft apartment. Sarah Delaney worked on the interior design, and with a palette of white walls, limed wood and ebonised mid-century-style furniture she created a dynamic yet monochrome colour scheme.

Above – Kitchen: We created a kitchen and dining area off the main living room, with a smart Bulthaup kitchen designed by Colin Astridge, and chairs by B&B Italia around the dining table. A signature MB wood burning stove by Rais was installed – even though the property has underfloor heating throughout, these are amazingly economical and heat up the space in no time. Three sets of sliding doors open out onto the garden.

Top, right – Landing stairwell: As always, the need to introduce more light into the space was paramount, and the solution was to place a huge rooflight above the stairs and long rooflights above the first floor corridor with walk over glass panels on the ground floor ceiling to bring south light into this predominantly north facing building. The use of glass 'balustrades' for the staircase, with a mirror hung on the wall opposite, is another clever device to maximize the light effect.

Right – Bathroom: One of three bathrooms, the master bathroom uses mirrors to maximise the light coming from the rooflight above.

Battersea Power Station Apartments

London SW8

Architect **Wilkinson Eyre**
Interior Design **Michaelis Boyd**
Masterplan Architect **Rafael Vinoly**

THE BRIEF: Battersea Power Station, now Grade II* listed, was erected in the Thirties to a design by Sir Giles Gilbert Scott, and expanded after the Second World War. It is one of the largest brick buildings in Europe (the footprint of St Paul's Cathedral would fit in the boiler house) and one of London's most recognised and beloved structures. The original architect allegedly wanted square brick chimneys but unusually was overruled by the client because round chimneys increased the efficiency of the power turbines.

After being decommissioned in 1983, its future was uncertain. Several redevelopment plans failed to materialise and, there were fears that it would be demolished. In 2012, a consortium of Malaysian investors comprising SP Setia, Sime Darby and the Employees' Provident Fund purchased the 42 acre site. Their vision was ambitious: a complete restoration of the Power Station, to include the construction of nearly 4000 new homes, 1.25m sq. ft of offices, 700,000 sq ft of retail, new hotels and an entertainment district, as well as fantastic new transport facilities.

We were invited to present our ideas for the residential interior architecture for 254 luxury flats in phase two of the development where we would be working with architects Wilkinson Eyre Associates.

Left: This is a computer-generated image of how the gardens around the developments will look. They provide both an elegant vista and a refuge.

Above: Some apartments are within the existing fabric of the turbine halls either side of the boiler house and the new build apartments sit on top of both the turbine halls and the boiler house. The latter will frame a new two and a half acre roof garden. Two slightly different looks are offered, reflecting the fact that Battersea Power Station was built in two stages, pre- and post-war. Our vision was for some of the apartments to be "edgier" than other prestigious developments, using distressed materials such as unlacquered brass, large freestanding baths and handmade tiles to reflect the history of the building.

We built a show flat on the top of the western turbine hall, showcasing all the high-spec materials we would be using, together with a range of custom-made furniture prototypes from Paul Smith, Tom Dixon and other leading designers. The view over the River Thames is spectacular, it is a pity this flat will be dismantled, we would rather like to live in it ourselves.

"Our designs were industrial-authentic,
highly tactile and visually dramatic."

So much inspiration came from the architecture of the building itself, we want to make sure the owners feel part of its heritage, not alienated in a beige modern box. These are not standardised interiors, these are based on something that's historically truthful, both to the richness of the period and the building. The emphasis here is on combining a raw industrial edge with craftsmanship and tactile materials.

Always conscious of the building's industrial past, we are using a great deal of Crittall glass and metal screens within the flats, not highly polished and homogenised but authentic in feel. They are unusual, more what you would see somebody's house rather than a development. We are committed to providing a particular touch, showcasing chairs by Jean Prouve for example.

While both apartments are different in terms of look both are finished to the same high standards. Apartment 1 (Heritage '33) is inspired by pre-war design.

Kitchens: Simple theatre-style kitchens, using concrete work surfaces, unlacquered brass taps, chevron antiqued wood flooring and open plan dining areas are shown here in the Heritage 33 style. Paint colours are darker and in tune with the materials rather than making a statement by themselves.

Bathroom: The free standing William Holland bateau copper bath, the herringbone marble floor and intricate, Art Deco inspired tiles plus brass tap and light fittings create a richness and warmth that is also contemporary.

Above: bathrooms: The idea was to make each space unique for the homeowner. The apartments are all different in their layouts. Here are the bathrooms for Heritage 46, post war inspired, using lighter more contemporary colours, and the same luxury specifications.

Dining rooms/sitting rooms/kitchens: The inspiration for much of our designs came from the huge windows. Some of the apartments are double-height duplexes, and we were excited about building some amazing staircases which will be in tune with the aesthetic of the building.

Chapter 2
Houses in the Country

Kingham House
Kingham, West Oxfordshire

Architect **Michaelis Boyd**
Interior Design **Sarah Delaney**
Landscape Design **Jinny Blom**

THE BRIEF: We first met Liz and Simon Dingemans when Liz approached us about their country house, a stunning William and Mary building in one of Oxfordshire's most beautiful villages. Grade II* listed, Pevsner praised it as 'one of the finest small houses of this date'. Liz had seen our work for Babington House, private members club and country house hotel in Somerset - and felt the two properties had a great deal in common, both being of handsome proportions with a family feel.

The house, which used to be the Old Rectory, required major restoration as it had not been done up since it was sold by the church to the previous owners in 1985. The family had lived in the house for a couple of years before work began, even though everything was on its last legs. As well as restoring the main house the Dingemans also wanted the barn rebuilt and a tennis court and swimming pool installed in the grounds.

Left: The beautiful Grade II* listed rear elevation with the new stone conservatory that was granted planning permission to house the large modern open plan family kitchen; this new extension was on the site of the old dog kennels.

The new extension creates a wonderfully light filled space for the kitchen with very long views over the fields. This is the only room that has a stone floor with underfloor heating and is the hub of family life. There are French doors and sash windows to each elevation and the kitchen leads into the Jinny Blom designed garden that takes you to the barns, swimming pools and tennis court.

In the main house we had contemporary radiators modelled to a period design, restored the classical features in the ceilings, cornicing and panelling and gave a new lease of life for the original floorboards. London-based interior designer Sarah Delaney helped Liz decorate with a mix of vintage and contemporary furniture and lighting to give the house a modern yet comfortable atmosphere.

Opposite, top: The new extension is the perfect place for a modern kitchen. As always, we turned to the Bulthaup experts, Kitchen Architecture, to create a simple theatre style cooking and dining space. Designed along one wall and a central island, the wall houses a four-oven Aga while the island provides a sociable work area and is home to modern appliances and an additional smaller prep sink. The use of solid oak for shelving and worktops gives the area an organic, traditional feel and reflects the extensive use of wood throughout the house. The dining chairs were sourced from a local shop and had originally been church chairs – appropriate for a former vicarage.

Opposite, bottom: We all wanted to retain the wonderful panelling and were able to restore it to its former glory. All the floors were laid with reclaimed hardwoods, and the simple lines of the furniture and treatment of the curtains allow these to take centre stage.

Above right: A view of the original and restored William and Mary staircase, cornicing and wainscoting.

Eastcourt House
Wiltshire

Architect **Michaelis Boyd**
Interior Design **Sarah Stewart Smith**

THE BRIEF: The house, dating from 1658 and Grade II* listed in 1951, required a great deal of work because nothing had been done to it in over fifty years. But the building and setting was and is incredibly romantic. Surrounded by a thousand acres, with lawns rolling down to a lake and views as far as the eye could see, it needed to be lovingly brought back to life for Nicola and James Reed, their six children and guests. We were to work to a sensible budget that saw the money being spent on restoring what was there, rather than seeking to change the layout.

Eastcourt House was built in the years 1658-62 for Giles Earle, a colourful Whig politician, soldier and wit. Entirely self-made, Earle distinguished himself as a colonel attached to the Duke of Argyll and enjoyed a successful parliamentary career in Robert Walpole's government, not least for 'the coarseness of his humour which made him an acceptable companion in the minister's happier hours of social life'. Eastcourt remained in the Earle family for a further a hundred and fifty years after which it was bought by and sold to a succession of entrepreneurs, its last incumbent being Sir Isaac Pitman, inventor of shorthand. Now home to the Reed family, creators of the Reed Group, it is ironic to realise that by not housing a dynasty Eastcourt has nonetheless perpetuated a tradition lasting almost four hundred years.

As stated in the brief, the house had endured many alterations throughout its history. It was L-shaped, with a service wing at the east end on the north side. A large block incorporating a staircase hall to the north was built on the west side of the house in the mid eighteenth century: which retains its contemporary fittings. In 1773 the house stood in a small park with a lake to the south. In the nineteenth century the centre of the south front was extended and the south porch, dated 1658, was reset in the north front at the centre of a two-storeyed corridor built between the staircase hall and the service wing. Although the exterior was to be kept intact, and our main objectives were altering the interior layouts, planning permission dragged on for three years. At one point our clients asked other architects to apply, to see if this was merely ineptitude on our part. When they were rebuffed too, we all knew we were dealing with a very tricky individual at the planning office.

"Despite the project's sensitive restoration programme, it still took three years to obtain planning permission."

Above: Pevsner recorded this as the drawing room, and the carving of Giles Earle, his family, and the south front of the house are depicted on a wooden overmantel above the fireplace. Now the dining room, we kept the original panelling, replacing the window sashes and radiators.

Opposite: Eastcourt's front door is enclosed by an imposing, engaged Doric porch, with transomed-crossed mullioned windows on each side. These were a new invention in 1658, but needed a fair amount of restoration by the time the Reeds acquired the property.

Even if the facades left and right of the main block were added at different times, there is a romantic coherence which connects them. All we did was replace the twelve pane window frames, sashes and lintels, the slate tiles on the roof and make good the stone chimney stacks. With lawns rolling down to the lake we felt this was the most atmospheric house we had worked on.

Although we sought to change very little in the house, the local planning officer tried to refuse almost everything we suggested and demanded to be involved as if the house was hers. The original plan remained unaltered and early ideas to put in a grand staircase and big studio window were refused.

We worked very closely with interior designer Sarah Stewart-Smith who specialises in listed buildings and is not afraid to mix the antique with the contemporary. Her ideas for the dining room work brilliantly, for example putting Starck's witty Louis Ghost Perspex chairs with an antique dining table.

We persuaded James and Nicola to invest in an alternative energy system for the whole house and the estate cottages. A woodburning boiler, although expensive to install, is very economic over time. It uses wood chips from the estate that not only saves long-term costs of a conventional energy bill but also provides a carbon neutral solution. We were able to harness its powers to heat the new swimming pool we put in, as well as the estate cottages.

Opposite, top: Although most of the floors were beyond repair and were replaced with reclaimed oak, the pine floor in the drawing room was salvageable and wonderfully scored with years of stiletto heel marks. We restored all the beautiful old panelling in several rooms in the house.

Opposite, bottom: In country houses we almost always leave the bedrooms simply and classically designed, merely replacing or restoring the floorboards, windows and walls. We also found several classic mantelpieces under many layers of paint.

Above: The kitchen and informal dining room required a complete redesign. Two enormous skylights light the contemporary black and stainless steel Bulthaup kitchen from above. A side door leads out to a stone walled enclosed courtyard where dining can be enjoyed protected from the elements.

Left: Most of the bathroom fittings for Eastcourt came from The Water Monopoly in London, a company specialising in English and French reconditioned antique and reproduction bathrooms. This copper bath allows the bather a beautiful view over the back lawn and Wiltshire hills beyond.

"The pine floor in the sitting room was wonderfully scored with years of stiletto heel marks."

The Miller's House at Froe
Portscatho, Cornwall

Architect **Michaelis Boyd**
Landscape Design **Jinny Blom**

"This Cornish house appealed because there was water everywhere."

THE BRIEF: An obsession with the sea had seen publishing guru John Brown and his wife Claudia enjoying their house in the South of France for many years. But when they realised that most of their neighbours had become English and American holidaymakers they decided on a change of venue. This Georgian Miller's house in Cornwall appealed to them because of the water – it had a creek, lake, jetty and an extraordinary position looking across the estuary to St Mawes. But none of the rooms took advantage of this view. So we were asked to completely renovate the main house and turn it into a three bedroom home, as well as converting the adjacent studio space into bedrooms for the children; maximising the views as integral to the design.

Below: Jinny Blom, RHS Chelsea Flower show medallist, was brought in to relandscape the terracing and planting down to the lake (just visible in the picture). She installed wide slate terraces on two sides overlooking the creek and mill pool, with lawns below leading down to planted borders and the water's edge. Now you can arrive by boat at high tide and swim, canoe or kayak in the mill pool.

Opposite: At the back of the house, we added a balcony by inserting a steel cantilever into the house structure, and installed a seamless glass surround to make the most of the glorious views. We worked with contractors from the Trelowarren Estates, who sourced as much as they could locally.

"The Cornish planning officers actually seemed to like us and what we were trying to do. Which was rare."

Above: The huge, light filled kitchen, designed by Bulthaup with the Kitchen Architecture team, had sleek white units, a top-of-the-range steam oven and a big island unit.

Opposite, top: Permissions were granted to take out most of the wall at ground level and on the first floor looking down the estuary. In the kitchen and dining area we put in massive glass doors, which slide back into the wall. The grey limestone floor inside blends with the exterior basalt grey slate to create a seamless relationship between inside and outside. Big pendant lights reclaimed from the Rover car factory hang low over the oak Conran refectory table and Eames chairs. At the back you can see the Rais woodburning stove, Danish in origin and not cheap. However once installed, they are wonderfully effective and conventional heating hardly needs to be turned on.

Opposite, bottom left: We stripped out everything, exposing the roof and existing timbers to create this imposing master bedroom. There are two sets of sliding doors which lead onto a glass sided balcony so one can lie in both the bed and the bath to watch the tide ebb and flow in the creek. The second double bedroom has beautiful views over the garden and mill pool and a bathroom with slate basins and a slate sided bath. The third double bedroom has an en suite shower room.

Opposite, bottom right: Rooflights above the landing and staircase ensure that light falls all the way through to the ground floor, and an open plan doorway to the kitchen picture windows give a first glimpse of the creek.

Kintbury House
Kintbury, Berkshire

Architect **Michaelis Boyd**
Landscape Design **Veronica Mackinnon**
Lighting Design **Kate Wilkins**

THE BRIEF: Chris and Kate Dale had been living in this early Georgian (1714-1750) brick house for some years before deciding it needed renovating and bringing up to date. Hidden at the bottom of a narrow lane near Kintbury, the house had the classic architectural bones of the period, but several additions over the following centuries had disqualified it from any Grade listing. The key design brief was to make it a fantastic, contemporary living space for the Dales' three children and friends. As the interiors did not have official historical merit that needed preserving we were able to pursue a total refurbishment.

The Dales also wanted to apply for planning permission for a building to house a twenty five metre swimming pool. We put in an application for a contemporary cedar clad building.

Left and opposite: As shown, the exterior is a classic, redbrick, eighteenth century country house, but upon entering you're quickly spirited into the twenty-first century. The double height playroom has a mezzanine level leading to the main bedrooms and a fireman's pole suspended from the roof, which the children can slide down from their playroom attic space.

Overleaf: The large hallway doubles as a great place to play pingpong. Glass inserts in the roof with glass brick flooring at attic and first floor level bring daylight all the way down to the entrance hall. At the far end of the hall is the new, enclosed staircase which runs seamlessly from attic to ground level.

There is a room at each end of the cedar clad, grass roofed pool house, one used as Chris' study and the other as a gym and changing room. The pool can be used in summer or winter. Frameless glass sliding doors on the sides enable the kids to run from the garden to dive into the pool in the warmer months. We kept the interior very simple – a suspended Barrisol stretch ceiling and white walls. The pool has hand glazed pyrolave green tiles, similar to the ones we used in Soho House, Berlin and the red line of tiles down the middle delineate two swimming lanes. At twenty five metres the pool is half Olympic size.

"Glass sliding doors enable the kids to run from the garden to dive into the pool."

Praa Sands
Penzance, Cornwall

Architect **Michaelis Boyd**

THE BRIEF: Little Cottage was the very last seafront property along the line of the cliff at Praa, beyond which is nothing but sea, sand and rugged headland. Alex Michaelis had fallen in love with it when it was a rotting, overgrown 1950s cottage with no heating or electricity. Not only was it in a poor state, but the coastline it sits on is eroding and, surrounded by cliffs there are no means to move further back. The council planners told him he was 'completely mad' to want to build here, but Alex was now used to this. At first he was keen to restore the existing structure, but when the amount of asbestos discovered was deemed unsafe, the brief changed radically to full demolition.

The site was all about the views over the sea and the plan evolved from the idea of making the most of the views from the living spaces and the bedrooms. The construction is a super insulated pre-fabricated timber frame with an exterior render and an undecorated white skim coat on the interior, with insulating wild flower flat green roof.

"An eroding coastline was simply another obstacle to overcome."

GROUND FLOOR PLAN

1 - CHILDREN'S BEDROOM
2 - SNUG
3 - LIVING AREA
4 - KITCHEN
5 - WC
6 - UTILITY ROOM
7 - WET ROOM
8 - ENTRANCE
9 - BARBECUE AREA

FIRST FLOOR PLAN

1 - GREEN ROOF
2 - BATHROOM 2
3 - BEDROOM 2
4 - BEDROOM 3
5 - BATHROOM 3
6 - BEDROOM 4
7 - BATHROOM 4
8 - TERRACE

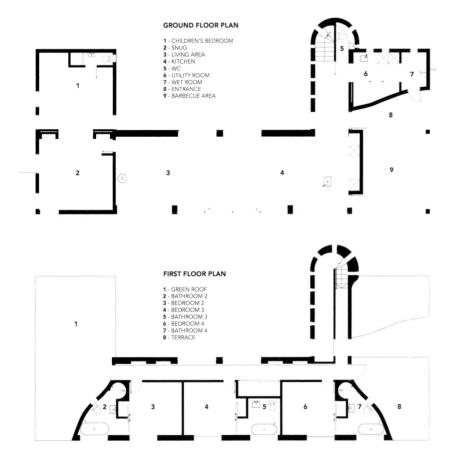

The ground floor consists of a downstairs shower/utility room that leads to an open staircase (based on a sea shell) spiralling within a curved core. This core has vertical slot windows that are lit at low level and rise up alongside the staircase. The stair core in turn drops down towards the front of the house into the kitchen/dining/ living area. Alex installed full height units to one end with an island in front. Not seen here, the living area was centred around a classic Rais wood burner as the heart and hearth of the building.

Like Oxford Gardens, this is a house for fun, but on a holiday scale. Beyond the living room is a games room, with steps leading up to a dormitory style room with bunk beds for children and a small ensuite bathroom.

The first floor is accessed by the shell staircase with a large circular skylight overhead. The double height stairwell then leads to a gallery landing with glazing to either end, one of which leads to a roof terrace. The corridor is lined with bookshelves either side of a fixed glass window with a long thin roof light overhead. There is a small gap between the corridor and the external wall, creating a band of light to the living area below, seen best after dark.

Off the corridor there are three bedrooms, all with full height glazing that slides into pockets, opening up the rooms towards the beach. Each bedroom has an ensuite bathroom with a cast iron bath by the window, giving views out to sea. The bathrooms also have circular showers, with porthole skylights overhead.

Duntisbourne House
Gloucestershire

Architect **Michaelis Boyd**
Landscape Design **Tom Stuart-Smith**

THE BRIEF: Our clients were relocating to the UK from Chicago, and fell in love with this classic Cotswold house near Cirencester. At the time their children were yet to be born, once it was finished they had produced four! We were asked to design a family friendly home, with all the usual modern up-to-date amenities, in anticipation of the children's arrival. The project was rolled out in four phases: first the gatehouse, then the conversion of the stable block into an office, nanny apartment and guest house followed by a new build pool and pool house, and finally the main house.

Above: The front elevation of the house shows the major structural work of moving the steps from the middle of the terrace to the left hand side. Just seen is the new wing built to house the kitchen and basement games room. A new roof, window sash frames and stone repointing were all part of the restoration programme.

Hallway, stair detail and outside view of staircase through window:
One of the main disappointments of the original house was the entrance, which forced one to turn right and climb a tiny kitchen staircase squeezed into a corner. We were happy to redesign the hallway and new staircase to create a strong and spacious statement.

The house was originally built in 1760 for Sir Mark Pleydell, who chose a 70-acre site high on the hill looking south-west across the valley to the village of Edgeworth. Alterations were made in 1800, in the 1920s and then again in 1971. Altogether over the centuries it has been knocked down, rebuilt, burned, reduced in size and, despite its grand façade, was surprisingly poky inside. The house remained empty for two years while we applied for the right permissions, which included dealing with a colony of bats – a protected species – in the roof of the main house.

We began by lowering all the floor levels by nearly two feet to increase the head height. We then opened up the whole house and introduced a big glass roof that brings light in to the ground floor, and also helps to locate oneself on entering. Then we added a new ground floor and basement wing for the kitchen and games room. After that we turned our attention to the pool house, a complete new build that still had to mimic the architecture of the stable block and main house. We managed this by designing a hierarchy of buildings that ended at the pool. We put in stone gables at each end of the pool house, and clad it in zinc and timber slats that pass over the glazed elevation. We worked closely with the highly acclaimed landscape designer Tom Stuart Smith who created the incredible vegetable gardens, as well as re-landscaping the main grounds.

"Despite our client's success in electronic trading, his Feng Shui expert forbade any form of wifi in the main house."

Opposite - kitchen and basement: Our clients were particularly inspired by Belgian design, and most of the kitchen materials were sourced from there. Crittall glass doors open out from the basement games room straight into the garden.

Top left - stable block: These buildings were fully restored externally and inside were converted into offices and a guest apartment where our clients stayed while work to the main house was completed. They loved it there, particularly the children who enjoyed riding on the site diggers.

Top right and above - pool house: A modern take on an agricultural barn building, emphasized by its surrounded vegetable plots. The pool house contains a fully equipped kitchen, making it easy to pick a salad and have it for lunch.

Overleaf: The new kitchen/basement extension and pool house are photographed at night. In particular the new drystone walls were faithful replicas of the originals and help to successfully integrate the new buildings with their surroundings. It seemed as if they had always been there.

Oxfordshire Manor House
West Oxfordshire

Architect **Michaelis Boyd**
Interior Design: **Sarah Delaney**
Landscape Design **Jinny Blom**

THE BRIEF: Our clients had been looking for a weekend country house for some time, and while in London they had been happy to buy a high quality development, this time they were keen to create an environment with a more personal feel for themselves, their children and weekend guests. This Grade II listed manor house, in an ancient Oxfordshire village, seemed perfect, but it was in a tired state. Their project manager advised simply updating the thirteen bathrooms but inevitably the job grew as we unravelled the house.

Above: The back elevation of the house showing the beautiful greenhouse extension – already in situ and listed. The garden links the pool with the main house.

Above – dining room and library: The previous owners had opted for pale, neutral colours throughout and we largely kept to this theme, except for the library, which had been a dark red but was brought up to date with a deep blue. Reclaimed oak lightened the interiors, replacing the dark brown, scarred wooden floors we originally found, both upstairs and down.

Left: The wine cellar was a particular source of pride. Transformed from a crumbling dank basement into a state of the art temperature controlled 'cave', it is protected by Crittall glass doors leading into the tasting room.

A property had existed on this site since 1204 when the manor was among several granted to the Cistercian Beaulieu Abbey. It was surrendered to the Crown during the Dissolution of the Monasteries in 1538 and subsequently held by the Bourchier and Perrott families before coming to Charles Ponsonby, 2nd Baron de Mauley in 1860, whose family already feudally owned the village.

Extensive remodelling over the centuries did not inspire Pevsner who noted that the house was 'a patchwork which fails to be picturesque'.

Inheriting a 'patchwork' worked in our favour as it meant we virtually had carte blanche to redesign the interiors, opening them up to let in more light. Our clients also wanted to install a pool and pool house, and the challenge was to re-landscape the plain green lawns into a garden that sat well between the old house and the new. A busy main road had caused the previous owners to create a great mound of earth and rubbish from other sites to muffle the noise, therefore an entire re-landscaping of the garden was necessary. We decided to take this opportunity to install a large wood chip boiler to reduce heating costs. We were happy to be working once more with Sarah Delaney on the interiors and Jinny Blom on the gardens, whose vision is so similar to our own.

Opposite - entrance hall and top of stairs landing: Light was reintroduced by the first floor rooflight through the entire staircase to the entrance hall. Not many rooms retained fixtures or fittings that were of historic value, except for the lovely arched windowpanes and ceiling cornices.

Above - bathroom: One of the thirteen bathrooms in the house, we made sure each one looked unique, with reclaimed fixtures and fittings.

Above right-sitting room: Reclaimed timber flooring was laid throughout the house, to add warmth to the cool neutral tones of the walls and furnishings. The sitting room on the ground floor looks out over the garden towards the pool.

"This was a 14 bedroom house that had been built up piecemeal over the centuries."

Pool house: This was built with dry stone walling in the same Cotswold stone as the main house and timber shingled roofing that turns grey with time, and exposed internal oak beams.

Jinny Blom's challenge here was to create a private garden between the house and pool that worked with both traditional and contemporary buildings.

Below: Our clients have a superb collection of vintage cars, so we built a new garage space and decided to expose the oak trusses to add some theatre to the experience.

Chapter 3
Places People Go To

Babington House
Frome, Somerset

Architect **Michaelis Boyd with Simon Morray-Jones Architects**
Interior Design **Ilse Crawford, Susie Atkinson**

THE BRIEF: When we first approached Babington House with Nick Jones along its meandering, tree-lined drive, we all knew that this country house could be a great success. We had previously worked for the owner Nick Jones on his original Soho House club in London's Greek Street, and some years later, he consulted us about this new venture: to redefine the country house hotel.

Nick wanted the experience of Babington to be like staying in your own home, where you could eat, drink and play whenever and wherever you wanted, but without having to lift a finger. It was an exciting venture as well as a big investment – he even asked Alex to take part of his fee as shares to show his belief in the project!

The main house was to be used for bedrooms, kitchen, restaurant and bar, with the coach house and outlying buildings given to a swimming pool, spa, gym, cinema, the hotel reception and additional accommodation. There was also a walled garden, an 18th century chapel and a lake. It was a huge project, certainly the biggest we had ever undertaken at the time.

The main house is mainly Georgian, Grade II* listed and was built in 1705, although a manor house has been recorded on the site since 1572. It had belonged to a family before the Soho House group bought it, and so historic details, such as plasterwork, were kept, as well as the original doors, staircases and fireplaces.

Having worked with Nick before, we knew how he went about things and predictably, the project started to go over budget, so little luxuries like

oak floors were downgraded to pine, and colossal baths were reduced in size. Somehow, though, Nick managed to renegotiate all the deals he had made to stick to his original plan.

Opposite: The church of St Margaret's, which is Grade I listed, faces the front of its Grade II* partner. The church no longer hosts regular services but is licensed for weddings in conjunction with Babington House.

Above: The library in the main house, showing the restored original wood panelling and stripped pine floors, provides a quiet place for reading and relaxing. The talented Susie Atkinson who specializes in quirky, individual and colourful rooms revamped all the interiors at Babington.

"When we first approached Babington House along its meandering, tree-lined drive, we knew that this was a project for us."

Getting planning permission was probably the trickiest aspect of the project, as the last hotel that the local council had approved remained unfinished and in ruins, and they didn't want the experience repeated. Vital to our success was working with the best local people. We were really fortunate to be helped by the Bath architect Simon Morray Jones, whose inside knowledge proved invaluable when it came to dealing with the planning office. Having Ilse Crawford on board, and then later, Susie Atkinson, in charge of the interiors gave Babington its beautiful design edge.

This project was a steep learning curve for us. We had no experience designing hotels, and neither had Nick, and we certainly didn't get everything right. However, we did set a new standard in hotel design and service. The atmosphere is relaxed and informal, the look glamorously shabby. The end result after 18 months was a private country house feel with a modern, urban twist, as far removed from high-end hotels' version of country living as you can imagine. The model obviously worked – we've lost count of the number of times since this project that clients have asked for their design to be like Babington.

Opposite, above: Working with Nick, as well as with his friends the film producer Eric Fellner and the entrepreneur Robert Devereaux, was unbeatable. Their experience of staying in top hotels all over the world was invaluable. Each room was individually designed and much more spacious than is standard, but it was the bathrooms that set Babington's accommodation apart. We put baths inside the bedrooms and also installed enormous walk-through showers; both ideas were radical at the time. We had first designed these for our Clarendon Road project the year before, where Nick saw them and earmarked them for Babington.

Opposite, bottom left: The coach house was prime for converting into bedrooms, and it was here that we had the most fun because no planning permission was required to realise our designs. We took advantage of the building's height, introducing sleeping platforms so that each of the twelve rooms would be on two levels, with a seating area below and open staircases leading up to the beds.

Opposite, bottom right: The famous Babington bar, a recreation of a Parisian 'zinc', which guests have admitted 'inspires an incredible capacity for drunkenness' and which has decadence nailed into its very joints..

Right, above and below: Meanwhile, out of the barn we created a high-tech cinema, complete with raked seating. The cowshed was converted and extended to hold the indoor pool and massage rooms. Running alongside is a heated outdoor pool.

Pizza East
Shoreditch, London

Architect **Michaelis Boyd**

THE BRIEF: The day after Nick Jones opened his East London members club Shoreditch House in June 2007 it was packed to full capacity day in and day out. The area was booming, techies and hipsters were moving in, the stock market was up and everyone was having a good time. So the following year he decided to create Pizza East: well-cooked, simple food in surroundings that were raw and industrial yet warm and welcoming at the same time. Not a members club, but a place that anyone could eat at. Which was just as well, for when we launched in 2009, in the teeth of the worst recession anyone could remember, the queues ran round the block.

Left: With an area of 5,700 sq. ft, seating 170 and housed on the ground floor of the Tea Building on the corner of Shoreditch High Street and Bethnal Green Road, Soho House Group's Pizza East replaced the old Tea Bar.

Opposite: The interior architecture shows respect for the building's industrial roots, with concrete walls and exposed beams, pipes and columns. The main entrance is through the original Tea Building staircase lobby with all original tiles and concrete left exposed. A white tile reception desk greets guests as they enter the main space through the original warehouse doors.

main feature central bar. Two long reclaimed factory tables with swivel stools sit between the main bar and pizza bar and private dining room.

The fabric of the building suited raw industrial relaxed seating. Few new materials were used: brick was left as brick, block left as block and concrete as concrete. All tiles were cleaned and uncovered. The only new material that was introduced was a timber floor to soften the range of materials, where the floor had been old dark concrete tiles. Preserving them would have made the space feel too cold and dark, as all the other surfaces were hard. The timber used, however, was made of old scaffolding planks so it felt original.

Pizza East was inspired by the very relaxed and trendy Los Angeles pizza concept, *Pizzeria Mozza*, where they use a unique recipe and 'wood-fire' their pizzas. It was felt that the wood-firing process had to be very visible, as pizza-making itself is a visual process, with all that comes with the the throwing of the dough. With that in mind, the open kitchen was originally conceived to be in the middle of the restaurant so that you could see the pizza-making process from the street but this was impractical as it would have taken up to much seating space in a prime area of the restaurant.

Above: We created an open plan restaurant which comprised various areas: a waiting high table with bar and retail deli area, a central seated bar with drinks, cheese and meat display, a private dining area and a pizza bar with view over the kitchen and pizza ovens. The mixed timber and zinc tables with old school chairs were loosely placed around the

Opposite, top: We kept the palette of materials simple to compliment the existing structure. White crackled tiles with green bands for the bar and pyrolave stone above, echo the original green capping tile in the building entrance. New concrete plinths were cast on site, with a chamfered edge detail, in keeping with the existing columns' detail, to hold a large timber-top table. Leather buttoned banquette seating was added to the perimeter to add comfort and soften the space. Reclaimed antique lights were installed with all pipes, ducts and conduits left exposed in ceiling.

Opposite, bottom right: We created a smaller drinking and eating bar in the centre of the space, inside the experience. This was complimented by a variety of eating places: private dining, drinks bar and a 'table bar' with beer pumps at one end, to create a more casual interaction and to stimulate and entertain

"This will probably be seen to have been the most successful and influential restaurant opening of 2009."

Giles Coren

Soho House Los Angeles
9200, Sunset Boulevard

Architect **Michaelis Boyd**
Interior Design **Vicky Charles, Soho House Design**

THE BRIEF: Since 2005, Soho House had been running its highly successful 'pop-up' headquarters during Oscar week, drawing considerable cachet amongst a highly sophisticated crowd because of its 'no expense spared' approach to the interior design, location, food and service. People were dazzled by it, and following the successful opening of both Soho House New York and a Cecconi's restaurant on the former Morton's site on Melrose Avenue, the plunge was taken to open a fully

fledged, permanent member's club on Sunset in the spring of 2010.

The chosen site was a bland glass office block, originally constructed by the Luckman family in 1964, to which Charles Luckman added a penthouse in 1971. In 2009, the late, great architect Stephen Kanner completed a multi-million pound overhaul, including re-cladding and re-skinning the exterior and upgrading the interior space. Another reason to install a Soho House at the top was (and is) its location for top entertainment companies such as Ford Models, Abrams Artists, Atlas Entertainment and Media Talent amongst others. Perfect for a Soho House in the 20,000 sq foot penthouse above them.

The 360 degree penthouse views were incredible, looking out over the city from the terrace bar both at night and during the day.

At the beginning, concerns were raised that Los Angeles was not traditionally a members club culture, and on top of that, how would potential members be enticed into the building, through a garage and up a dedicated lift? The solution was to create an even more unique and special experience, which was partly why we were called in. What was not required was the usual LA sleek and modern look; in this very bleak, square space we needed to inject comfort, warmth and quirkiness. Vicky Charles was the designer responsible for that worn, eclectic, mid century modern look while we went to work on breaking up the space to create a series of distinct, relaxing yet glamorous spaces.

Unlike the rest of the group's outposts, no pool was installed, because the building could only sustain a depth of 4.5 ft, plus we were told there was no need to have a pool because everyone in Los Angeles has one at home. This was a reasonable point, so for the top floor we designed an interior/exterior garden with a retractable roof and pond in the middle, to create an extraordinary dining space, which opens onto the Sky bar terrace. On this floor we also designed a space for the Sky private dining room. On the floor below, named the Club floor, we designed space for a billiards room, private bar and lounge, and study. Today, more than five years later, Soho House L.A is so oversubscribed that Nick has found a second outlet in downtown L.A's Arts District, and plans to open in a year's time.

"This Sunset Boulevard eyrie has become the entertainment industry's favourite club."

Opposite, top: In the members' bar, Old Hollywood glamour with allusions to an English gentleman's club create a welcoming atmosphere, and still with that amazing view.

Opposite, bottom left: The Sky restaurant on the top floor, with Vicky Charles' unexpectedly fully grown olive trees that were airlifted onto the roof. Hanging lanterns create an almost innocent party atmosphere.

Opposite, bottom right: We designed this curved, sweeping Hollywood staircase as a tribute to the golden age of film, made of beautiful oil rubbed bronze, stone and glass.

Right, above and below: In both the billiard room and the bathrooms, we made sure that the view was the main focus.

Soho House Berlin
Torstrasse, Mitte, Berlin

Architect **Michaelis Boyd**
Interior Design **Susie Atkinson**

THE BRIEF: As the Soho House Group grew, so did our working relationship, to a point where we could list Babington House, the Electric in Notting Hill, Pizza East and Soho House in LA (see previous pages) as unique collaborative achievements. A local developer had persuaded Nick to take a look at a building – and within ten minutes he'd decided to take it. It was built in 1928 by the Jewish Jonas family, was a department store, then the home of Hitler Youth, before it became the East Germany Communist Party HQ. After German reunification the building has been legally returned to the descendants of the Jonas family, but had remained derelict. Its state of repair and powerful history meant that the local community was particularly interested in its fate.

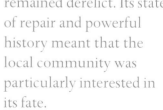

Left: The building had been adapted through various phases of history: Original 30s art deco shape and details were followed by a more fascist aesthetic and yet later less interesting additions in the 60s under communism.

Opposite: 'Grit with glamour' was our brief, and the reception desk delivers that message straight-away, being constructed from scaffolding with professional stage lights suspended above.

The original concept was to borrow from the authentic German style of the 30s: Art Deco, Bauhaus and de Stijl mixed with iconic Soho House relaxed glamour. The style currently favoured in German interior architecture is pared down, industrial and gritty. The guiding phrases for Soho House Berlin was 'faded grandeur'.

Working together with the Berlin practice JSK and Susie Atkinson, the building fabric would be honest, textural and understated in order for the glamour not to be too theatrical, with much of the brickwork and concrete exposed. New concrete floors were poured and new parquet floors laid, true to the original pattern and dimensions and aged to look like the original parquet, which had been destroyed by flooding. There were also old ceilings made of square terracotta tiles, but unfortunately due to new building regulations these had to be covered.

At the very start an extensive scouting process was embarked upon in order to define what was to be salvaged from each of the various eras of building's history. The idea was either use those exact elements or to replicate them within the new build. A good example is the old 1930s die-cast wheels found as part of the basement workshop, formerly used as stopcocks for pressure valves. These became the thermostatic mixers for the basement showers. On an upper floor were found 1930s tap crossheads that were tooled and used as the basis for a new range of taps completely unique to the building. There was a door handle design that was sadly not used due to a minimum thickness required by building regulations aimed at avoiding their melting in case of fire. All the tiling in the basement remained 1930s cream crackled brick tiles. These were salvaged, then sent away to be matched and used for all bathrooms. A cast was also made of the original Art Deco baths and the design used within certain club bathrooms.

The hotel bedrooms run over four floors in the mid-levels of the building and were segmented into four different styles, based on various bedroom and bathroom combinations including Classic (Lonsdale bath), Art Deco (Double bateau baths, for the largest rooms) and shower rooms for the Attic Bedrooms. Although there were four distinct characters to the hotel rooms, each was personalised so that guests would never feel as if they were staying in the same room twice.

Opposite: Another view of the reception area with giant circular staircase. The shark on the wall is by Damien Hirst, to whom Nick handed a can of paint at the opening party and asked, 'Can you do anything with this?'

Top: Berlin has a grey hardness about it, so Susie Atkinson's interior decoration choices for the bedrooms included abundant colour and comfort, using authentic 1930s colours and chintz fabrics popular at the time.

Above: In the bathrooms, crackle glazed cream tiles were recreated from tiling we found in the basement.

SOHO HOUSE BERLIN

"From Hitler Youth to Soho House."

The Club floor was given its own reception and designed to have distinct yet open areas. The kitchen restaurant, designed to be more relaxed than the publicly-accessible restaurant on the ground floor, flows into a cocktail 'glamour' bar in the centre, surrounded by banquette seating, snugs, dining and a games lounge. All was conceived as one big space, although each part achieves a different feel.

The eighth floor was a new build extension on top of building and had a very different character to the rest of it. Wall-to-wall glazing was used so that guests would be struck by the incredible views over Berlin. White Carrera marble was used for the bar but with a ridged design, inspired by the 1930s. The swimming pool was made of pyrolave, a French volcanic lava stone which is inert so a crackle glaze can be fired onto the stone without it breaking, giving the effect that the tiles are original. As bright colours were very fashionable in the 30s, emerald green was chosen and influenced the whole of the eighth floor.

Opposite, top: A grittier version of Cecconi's restaurant in London (also owned by Nick Jones), the circular banquette seating encloses a circular bar in the centre of the room.

Opposite, bottom: Screening rooms are central to the ethos of the Soho House Group. When Nick opened in Soho he catered initially to the film industry that provided the core of his members.

Below: The Spa was divided into two areas: Cowshed Active with its fitness classes, Techno Gym equipment and personal trainers, and Cowshed Relax, home to four comfy manicure and pedicure chairs, private treatment rooms, relaxation pods, a sauna, steam room and a spacious Hamam.

Bottom: The top floor open air swimming pool, heavily influenced by 1930s design and used all year round with views of the information tower.

Soho Farmhouse
Great Tew, Oxfordshire

Architect **Michaelis Boyd with Alex Jackson, Soho House Design**
Interior Design **Vicky Charles, Soho House Design**
Landscape Design **Portus and Whitton**

THE BRIEF: We were delighted to be asked to work with the in house design team to prepare an initial planning document and architectural drawings for some of the final buildings at Nick's latest venture, a second English countryside retreat for Soho House in Great Tew, Oxfordshire. Nick Jones has assembled an in house team of contractors, designers and architects who can work exclusively on realising his vision. Tracey Farm was a derelict Cotswold farmhouse on Nick Johnston's beautiful Great Tew estate. The idea was to create a countryside escape of 40 individually designed cabins, assembled around the original farm buildings and complemented by the addition of contemporary new buildings. To include a restaurant, deli, cowshed spa and boathouse with indoor/outdoor pool.

Left: Soho Farmhouse is set on an 100 acre site. The project has expanded from its conception to include a Josh Wood Salon, four astro tennis courts, a winter ice rink, crazy golf, stables, an Electric Cinema, five a side pitch, gym and event barn.

Above: As many features as possible were reintroduced to preserve a farmhouse feel. A balcony and glazed canopies were added to allow guests to enjoy al fresco views over the courtyard and the lake toward the Boathouse and Gym. Use of cobbled flooring and distressed furniture all enhance the farmyard experience.

Right: The two mezzanine floors in the Main Barn overlook the central bar and dining area. On the flank walls, large glazed screens were incorporated to allow uninterrupted views out on the East-West axis and to let morning and evening light to flood into the central space.

Initially a 'prototype' cabin was built and furnished at Babington House, even though the built cabins, which are strung out along the small river Dorne are unique and very different in décor. The in house design team, led by Alex Jackson, based the ideas on a North American cabin structure, with small windows to the front, basic timber planking and a simple corrugated roof and then mixed this up with more modern and varied materials. Each cabin is equipped with a cabin supplies unit and the Farm Shop supplies fresh takeaway food and other goodies so if you want, you can spend all day in the cabin.

Opposite: The interior of the pool hall in the Boathouse was designed to replicate the feel of a working boathouse.

Top: The external timber cladding and internal wall lining to the pool hall and all common areas in the Boathouse were from original timber cladding salvaged from a demolished barn in Poland.

Above: The heated indoor pool extends to an uncovered outdoor pool that appears to float within the lake. The specialist pool finish was selected to resemble the Cotswold stone prevalent in the surrounding buildings.

Left: The bank of the original Mill Pond has been transformed into an island where the blackened timber-clad Steam and Sauna pavilion and shingle-clad Ice Room sit comfortably amongst the existing trees.

Byron Restaurants

Byron Islington, Upper St, London N1
Byron One New Change, Cheapside, London EC2
Byron Haymarket, Haymarket, London SW1Y
Byron Strand, The Strand, London WC2R
Byron Oxford, George Street, Oxford

Architect **Michaelis Boyd**
Interior Design **Clare Nash**

THE BRIEF: We were asked by Tom Byng to design the first Byron burger restaurant on High Street Kensington in 2007, with a very clear mandate: if it were to develop into a chain, it would be an 'anti-chain' chain. Each site would be designed according to the building, the geography, the audience and the zeitgeist, so that it felt part of the neighbourhood, as an independent restaurant would. High Street Kensington, which we managed on a very tight budget, was a great success and Byron is now a successful business encompassing 55 restaurants across the UK. To show the broad range of the Byron design ethos, we have selected five of our favourites, and we should mention the highly talented retail designer Clare Nash, with whom we collaborate on each and every one.

BYRON ISLINGTON

This was the seventh site we had worked on for Byron and for a number of reasons we really started to look at things differently. Oddly the site in Islington had previously been a failed burger joint, part of a chain, we were in the teeth of a recession and our budgets were even tighter than before. No one felt particularly positive as we sat round the derelict site, until somehow the idea emerged deliberately not to finish it, and ask our contractors to make some parts of it look even worse. On most jobs you are pushing your team for that last 3% to make the finishes look amazing. This time we were – literally and to their utter disbelief – asking them not to bother.

Above and left: We opened up the ground and first floor with a large void, where the flooring was stripped away from the joists to leave the building structure exposed. Ironically the cost did not prove cheaper in the end, as each timber had to be cleaned and fireproofed, while exposed lighting had to pass health & safety.

Opposite: The idea to put the Byron signage over the front and the windows was both effective and illegal, but we got the brand name out there before the Council caught up with us.

BYRON ONE NEW CHANGE

The acclaimed Modernist architect Jean Nouvel had been commissioned to redesign the outdated 1950s building opposite St Paul's, in the City of London, transforming it into a major office and retail complex. Sixty shops and restaurants are located there, open seven days a week, and Tom felt a Byron would more than fit in. Here was a new challenge as the empty site was a glass modernist box, opposite Sir Christopher Wren's English baroque masterpiece. We needed to work out how to bring character into the space, and build an aesthetic that was mildly ecclesiastical in style, to pay homage – as Byron always does – to its local surroundings.

Nouvel's plans had already attracted criticism, for while he didn't necessarily acknowledge tradition, he paid careful attention to the immediate surroundings. One New Change is known as the "stealth building" for two good reasons. Firstly, this low, wide £500m behemoth,

has muscled its way into the City while – remarkably – being all but invisible from just a few streets away. Secondly, its design – or, at least, its faceted facade or skin – really does have something of the look of a US Air Force Northrop Grumman B-2 Spirit, or stealth bomber, whose folded surface makes it virtually invisible to radar.

Above: Taking the folded surfaces to heart, we aimed to replicate these as part of the ceiling interiors, which in turn, echoed the folds designed by Axis Mundi for Strasbourg Cathedral. Drawing it was a complex process. We had to string model it on site, and exaggerate the scale to pull in a proper perspective. The chandeliers were installed to enhance the feeling of height and scale, and the pendant lights were Perspex based on the shape of an inverted church candle.

Top right: An open view of the dining area shows that there are some similarities across each restaurant; an open kitchen, endless pendant lighting, vintage chairs, oversized clocks, a lot of salvaged materials and interesting loos. Our contribution to the latter was to have peaceful church music played in them.

Bottom right: We always try to incorporate as many banquettes as we can in every Byron we work on, but they are one of the most expensive items to make and fit. Here we designed extra height backs inspired by the bishops' thrones found in most Anglican churches. Apparently the high back was created to indicate 'authority derived directly from the apostles'. We hope the Byron diners feel the same way when they visit.

BYRON HAYMARKET

The Haymarket in 1720 was described as 'a spacious Street of great Resort, full of Inns, and Houses of Entertainment; especially on the West Side… The Market for Hay and Straw, here kept every Tuesday, Thursday and Saturday, makes it to be of good Account.' We found our site awkwardly situated in a 'tourist trap' surrounded by cheap steak houses, yet yards away from the Theatre Royal Haymarket, a listed John Nash building. We decided to make the most of the exterior, with its imposing colonnaded façade, by using serious, classical signage and awnings. Inside a more difficult proposition lurked, as the previous occupant had been a 'House of Entertainment' with pole dancing paraphernalia, birdcages, podiums and 3 metre high fibreglass horses. The space was challenging in that there were two very separate areas, a dark rear dining room and a light filled classical front room. Given the location we wanted a taste of British, which wasn't overtly touristy. The solution was to incorporate different elements of London history into the design - in a playful, modern way.

Left: The open plan theatre kitchen with mezzanine above was installed in the lighter front room, and the custom made bar front had 10,000 pearl buttons cast into resin, acknowledging London's Pearly Kings and Queens. The wallpaper was also custom made, showing quirky hand drawn London landmarks. To the right of the picture are our famous banquettes, this time upholstered in classic 1950s Tube train fabric.

Opposite, main image and bottom right: In the much darker back room, the London Underground system was referenced in a massive three dimensional chandelier-esque celebration of the Tube network, creating a feature out of the gloom that lit up and enlarged the space. Wallpaper featured graphic London destinations with 'Haymarket' highlighted in red to draw the eye and partner with the red aluminium tables, made from salvaged 1950s Tube seats. The banquettes at the back were upholstered in classic pinstripes, an acknowledgement of London's financial heartland.

Opposite, top right: The walkway to some very interesting loos, painted in bright London pillar box red and decorated with deliberately kitsch Coronation and Royal Wedding plates.

"Isn't everyone fed up with the increasing homogenisation of the British high street?"

BYRON HAYMARKET

BYRON STRAND

Adjacent to the Adelphi Theatre, our next West End venture had originally been built in 1886 as the Adelphi Restaurant by the Gatti Brothers (Anglo-Swiss entrepreneurs who owned the theatre). Grade II listed, its façade had changed very little, but inside it had had many incarnations, the last being an amusement arcade. What was beneath all the carpeting and dirt was incredible and informed our creative vision; we discovered the original mosaic flooring and marble walls. We decided to restore the interiors with the feel of a glamorous West End speakeasy or brasserie circa 1900, using plenty of brass, deep reds and mirrored walls.

Opposite: We originally wanted neon signage but Westminster planners preferred us to use a glowing outline only. We still think this looks glamorous.

Above: It took eighteen months to receive planning permission, as English Heritage needed to be consulted as we uncovered more architectural and decorative gems. In the end it was decided that we should create a shell structure for the mezzanine floor, theatre kitchen and lighting, so that nothing actually touched the walls and ceilings, preserving as much as possible. We constructed it chiefly in brass, to bring out the richness of the ceiling and walls.

Right: Looking up at the brass chandelier and wonderful mosaic ceiling.

BYRON OXFORD

Oxford was one of the first Byron restaurants outside London. We were lucky to be given a derelict 1930s shop in the centre that belonged to the council; they had not the funds to refurbish it. In exchange for a rent-free period, Byron offered a complete overhaul. Normally we would have 6 – 8 weeks to refit, as a shop needs to start generating income as soon as possible. Now we had a 24 week programme, so we gutted the building, demolishing large elements and rebuilding new structures within a constrained and historically sensitive site. The striking design took influence from an original butcher's shop fitted with reclaimed tiles and the rear showcased some beautiful reclaimed shelving and historic remnants of the previous building. The bar and kitchen were custom made from large panels of glazed volcanic stone.

Above left: Traditional butchers' shops from the 1930's always had a tiled entryway and sheer glass windows, to properly showcase the displayed and hanging produce inside.

Above: We wanted to bring a warmth into the space, which a tiled interior can often negate, so plenty of reclaimed wooden tables and chairs were sourced, with warm whites used on the walls. We put in a polished concrete floor, and saved money on the banquettes by keeping the backs wooden rather than padded (we tested these at the office and they were very comfortable).

Opposite, right: The black and white tables and banquettes here were a playful acknowledgement of Friesian cattle, and the idea to stack as much white crockery as possible on the reclaimed French library shelving and white tiles hinted at the cleanliness and simplicity of a dairy.

Opposite, above right: The now classic Byron theatre-style kitchen has been refined over the many other outlets we have worked on, and is now the hub of the restaurant creating a buzz and warmth that is quintessential to the ethos.

Tom Aikens
Canary Wharf & Istanbul

Architect **Michaelis Boyd**

THE BRIEF: We had worked with Tom before on both Tom's Kitchen in Cale Street and the transformation of the Admiralty Restaurant in Somerset House, so we were very familiar with his vision. This was and is, of relaxed, comfortable, informal dining, in itself a showcase for Tom's commitment to fresh, ethically sourced ingredients using as many British suppliers as possible. Over the years, Tom has expanded his interests to include restaurants in St Katharine's Dock and Canary Wharf in London, and then an international flagship in Istanbul. We have been fortunate enough to work with him on all of them, and have selected Canary Wharf and Istanbul as two of the most recent and exciting projects.

TOM'S KITCHEN, CANARY WHARF, LONDON E14

A restaurant, bar and deli all in one, the location meant that during the week the site would enjoy a steady stream of business lunches and at the weekend, cater to a more laid-back brunch crowd. The space was enormous, seating 300, and unlike many of our other projects was a 1990s modern building, a blank box, and our challenge was to introduce all the character and warmth into it. We already had something of a blueprint from Cale St, where timber and tiles featured heavily, but we had to find the best way to break up the vast space.

Opposite: The main dining room itself was broken up in subtle ways, by partitioning spaces into disparate sections. We ran a poured concrete walkway along the centre, and broke up more space by using herringbone parquet flooring. A variegated use of tile patterns on the columns and a variety of pendant lamps also helped interest the eye.

Top, left: Another way to break up space was to pour a circular concrete floor and add a circular bar leading into the concrete walkway.

Top right: The Deli at Canary Wharf is very popular, providing breakfast and lunch for people on the go: we created a theatre style bar from Italian marble, showcasing delicious freshly baked bread and patisserie at eye level and within reach. A poured concrete floor and industrial designed pendant lights added to the feel of a creative, working kitchen space.

Above: For more private events, we created a private dining room, thus broadening the scope of choice for the restaurant's clientele.

TOM'S KITCHEN, ZORLU CENTRE, ISTANBUL

Tom was invited to bring his Kitchen concept to Turkey as one of a handful of upmarket yet informal European restaurants. We were delighted to be asked to design the restaurant at the chosen site, the Zorlu centre, created as Istanbul's first luxury shopping mall. It is a four-tower, five-function structure group, it comprises a public square, residential development and office space. There are over 200 designer shops and forty cafes and restaurants as well as a performing arts venue and a luxury hotel.

Bottom left: This was the first outpost of Tom's international business, so it was extremely important to get it right. Luckily our experience with Canary Wharf had made us familiar with fitting out a blank, modern canvas. We were allotted the centre's premier space, and divided the restaurant into two halves. Smoking is not banned in Turkey, so the right hand, outdoor section is for smokers.

Top left: We used many of the same ideas as in Canary Wharf, adapting only a few to suit the location. Herringbone parquet flooring, plenty of light warm wood and distinctive use of tiling patterns create a familiar yet chic environment in which to eat. We did however change the scale of the bar, as restrictions on the sale and consumption of alcohol have been tightened in recent years – 83% of Turkish people are teetotal. In keeping with Tom's commitment to using local, quality produce, we carefully sourced vintage photographs of local Turkish food suppliers.

Above: We used Crittall glass to surround the outdoor section, and put the herringbone parquet on the ceiling. We made almost everything with local craftsmen to preserve the integrity of the project.

Brewdog

Brewdog Shepherds Bush, London W12
Brewdog Clapham, London SW11

Architect **Michaelis Boyd**

THE BRIEF: In 2007 James Watt and Martin Dickie, two enterprising Aberdonians, bored with the industrial brewed lagers and stuffy ales that dominated the UK market, took matters into their own hands and started brewing their own craft beers. With controversial names like Punk IPA, Tactical Nuclear Penguin, Hardcore, Speedball and Tokyo – which, to the media's horror, they claimed was a binge drink cure – these enfants terribles' brewing philosophy was as exciting and dynamic as their beer. What also set BrewDog's founders apart from the masses was their distrust of venture capital and 'overbearing parent companies' when it came to raising finance. Instead they launched their own crowdfunding scheme, 'Equity for Punks', which raised millions, allowing BrewDog to expand rapidly and globally.

The company quickly branched out into operating bars, and we were fortunate to be selected to work on their design and fit out. It was clear from the start that there were elements similar to the Byron ethos, in that BrewDog was strongly anti-chain, but their requirement for a subversive, counter-culture vibe was far greater.

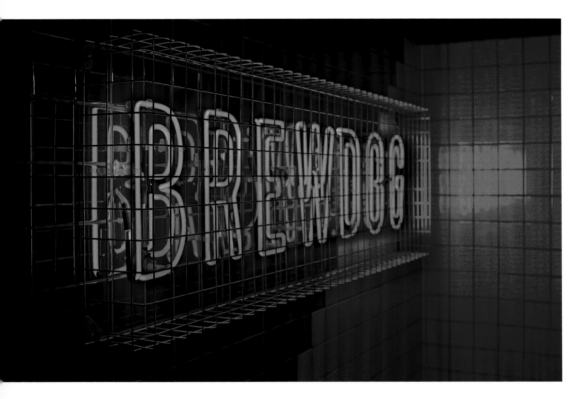

Left: All signage is carefully thought through, to let the customer know that 'Our bars are a beacon for craft beer. A focal point for the craft beer proletariat in our struggle with the industrial beer bourgeoisie...There will be nothing industrial or generic in sight, and this resolute philosophy extends to everything we serve.'

BREWDOG SHEPHERDS BUSH

Above: The Shepherd's Bush site was the first bar we designed for BrewDog. It was much larger than the Camden and Shoreditch bars, and we needed to retain the 'no-nonsense' style and match it with a more laid back vibe. We used plenty of exposed brick, iron and wood and created a cast concrete bar, which we decided would feature in all future restaurants. The number of beers on tap – over 40 – was unheard of, so we created a vast cinema display board for easy choice.

Right: We added comfort to the bar with different types of seating and lighting. Much of the lighting was sourced from cargo ships, particularly decommissioned North Sea boats, which kept the budget down.

> "The Thames was no barrier for us. We skimmed across like a stone, striking the beacon-lighting for craft beer south of the river." *BrewDog*

BREWDOG CLAPHAM

Clapham was the next location on BrewDog's list, their first in south London, and the fourth in Camden, Shoreditch and Shepherd's Bush. Clapham itself is largely residential, housing many young professionals and families, and so the brief was be slightly different – it needed to be distinct from the rough industrial palettes of the three previous bars to create a more polished drinking experience.

We designed different seating heights for the 120 seats: a mixture of comfortable banquette booths, informal seating and high tables to divide the space into five independent zones. We raised the ceiling to maximize the space and allow as much light as possible by day and fitted signature neon lights to set the mood for the evening. Texture and colour were key: the original timber and concrete floor was retained and graphic paint finishes, vibrant gloss colour tiles and lacquered surfaces run throughout the scheme. The feature bar front and walls were clad in triangular hand crafted wood in blues and oranges in a striking painted pattern to lift the space.

Opposite: A softer, more playful palette was required for Clapham, with the space broken up into distinct areas. The installation of the island bar tables was a first for the group.

Above right: Strips of fibreboard with different colour and width were used, softer looking than concrete, but also capable of heavy load bearing. Colour-blocking the bar was effective and fun.

Right: The different seating areas and types vary the space, above we sourced more salvaged ship's lighting.

The Williamsburg Hotel
Wythe Avenue & North 10th St, Brooklyn

Architect **Michaelis Boyd with KFA**

"Twenty years ago, if you saw someone running in MacCarren Park, it meant they were being chased. Now, Wythe is one of the hottest zip codes in the city."

THE BRIEF: Having seen our work in Soho House, Berlin, our New York clients approached us to design the building and interiors for a new hotel in Williamsburg.

The plan was to create a 150 room destination hotel. We were to collaborate with renowned New York architects, HWKN, who had gained planning permission for the envelope of this new build; we completely redesigned the exterior to reflect the industrial heritage of Williamsburg and added a water tower bar to the roof. We worked with the hotel management team who launched and operated legendary New York properties notably Ian Schrager's Gramercy Park Hotel, Andre Balazs's Standard Hotels and Sean MacPherson's The Bowery and The Jane Hotels. It was an incredible opportunity.

Another irresistible attraction was the neighbourhood. Williamsburg had long been home to the creative set who had left Manhattan in search of more space, which reminded us of London's Shoreditch with its similar industrial past and Bohemian present. As the bars, clubs, galleries and coffee shops sprang up, so interest from Manhattan's developers grew. The Williamsburg Hotel will build upon such pioneering outposts such as The Wythe and Urban Cowboy that celebrate North Brooklyn's gritty history, while quietly installing every modern convenience.

Our task for the building and interiors was to create a faded industrial feel, and with eight storeys, 150 bedrooms, double height ceilings and natural finishes to play with we looked to the past for inspiration. Images of crumbling or demolished hotels, factories and public buildings in Detroit, Philadelphia and Chicago helped us to slowly build up a profile of colours and materials. Past architects we were especially drawn to were Charles Noble, Louis and Paul Kamper and Louis Kahn. We noted that all the public rooms in these forgotten buildings were monolithic, with double height ceilings, decorated in Gothic, Romanesque or Empire styles, designed to impress and instill authority or awe. Behind these stage sets, the corridors to the guest rooms were wide and long, yet the bedrooms or offices themselves were modest. Bathrooms however, were usually the same size as the bedrooms, a luxury unknown in pre-Second World War America.

Prohibition was then in full swing, and we wanted to bring back a sense of that fun, danger and corruption.

Above: MB were in charge of designing this new build both externally and internally, with a brick, glass and Corten steel exterior. The building also houses a restaurant, rooftop pool, a grand ballroom and three distinct bars, including one in a replica water tower.

Opposite: The grand ballroom space boasts 30 ft ceilings and can accommodate up to 400 guests for events, galas and happenings. Light pours in via the Crittal glass ceiling; glamorous Murano glass chandelier lighting and wood parquet flooring is offset by the faded grandeur of the untreated walls.

Above: At the lower ground floor you enter this exclusive club via the back door. The underground bar perfectly realises that sense of a prohibited, clandestine drinking spot.

Above: Floor to ceiling windows offer breathtaking views of the Manhattan skyline and most bedrooms will have their own balcony. Our rendering shows a lot of natural wood to soften and warm the interior. The bathrooms will use sturdy, industrial fittings of aged bronze, and reflective Art Deco tiles.

The Groucho Club
Dean Street, Soho, London

Architect **Michaelis Boyd** with **Nicky Carter, Alice Anthony**

"I've had a perfectly wonderful evening, but this wasn't it." *Groucho Marx*

THE BRIEF: The Groucho was dreamed up in 1985 by a group of fifteen publishers, writers and agents who were sick of having nowhere to meet in London. The Garrick, the only members' club with a literary and thespian profile, had voted against female members, and half of the founders were women. Even before the doors opened membership became the Holy Grail of the London scene and in the last thirty years some truly memorable and hellraising parties have taken place in its private rooms. Peter Blake, Al Pacino, Bono, Oliver Reed, Damien Hirst, Madonna have all let their hair down, knowing that it was a place of safety where social media had yet to be invented.

Thirty years later, its new owner commissioned us to rework the site, which was a jigsaw puzzle of disparately sized rooms across three conjoined buildings, to create a unified space in which rooms could flow easily and intuitively without losing their sense of privacy. One enduring legacy of the club is its contemporary art collection, amassed from its creators in exchange for membership. Alison Watt, Jim Lambie, Tracy Emin, Gavin Turk, Mark Quinn, Gary Hume and Damien Hirst deserved an updated showcase for their extraordinary works. We collaborated with creative director Alice Anthony and the club's art director, Nicky Carter, on an overall theme to make the space look as if it had 'evolved over time', and not to eclipse the aura of the club with a complete overhaul. It took two years to complete.

Opposite: The Soho Bar on the first floor was a primary space where we took a more radical and far more contemporary approach to create a place ideal for working and networking, by day or night. The bar was given a new resin bar top with copper detailing, vibrant green lacquered walls and a reclaimed wooden floor from the BBC's Bush House. Tom Dixon designed the brightly upholstered furniture.

Above and top right: The Mary-Lou Room (named after Mary-Lou Sturridge, the former managing director of the club) on the first floor was reworked to create a new bar with a direct connection to the dining room. A reclaimed fireplace was installed while a feature plaster ceiling and shutters were added. Artworks include the pinstriped wall by Ian Davenport.

Right: The screening room on the second floor was a new addition, replacing the old snooker room. A double height skylight was installed to bring in more light for daytime events.

Overleaf: In the dining room, the walls were covered in grey linen to improve the acoustics, and features a restored plaster ceiling, luxurious Brazilian marble tables and curved banquette seating. The Groucho's impressive art collection, hung salon style, is a focal point in every room.

Kichwa Tembo Safari Camp
Masai Mara, Kenya

Architect **Michaelis Boyd with Nick Plewman Architects**
Interior Design **Fox Browne Creative**

THE BRIEF: We had got to know the Enthoven family well through our work for them on various projects. They half owned a small company of luxury, boutique safari lodges called andBeyond scattered across Africa. The lodges had been operating for many years, and were in need of updating and refurbishment. We were delighted when Joss Kent, andBeyond's CEO, asked us to work with Nicholas Plewman, resident architect, on a redesign of Kichwa Tembo. This was the first and best-loved Masai Mara camp, a hidden gem in the bush on the edge of the plains. Now hundreds of camps have sprung up as competitors, and we needed to deliver a radical revamp to beat the competition and propel the lodge into the 21st century. The camp was originally famous for being invisible, hidden in a rather reserved English way, so as not to disturb the animals. We wanted to retain that but add the possibility of Sundowners with a view, so we took the bold decision to move twenty-two of the twenty-eight tented rooms to the edge of the Mara. We kept the original communal buildings where they were, but with a mandate to open as many sides to their surroundings as possible.

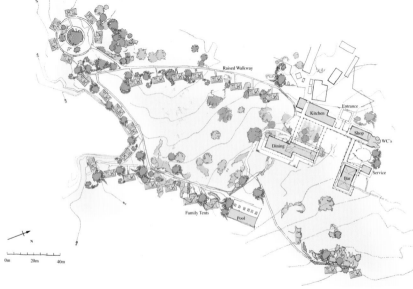

We demolished the existing tents and lodges, rebuilding the lodges using local stone, cypress wood walls and thatch. Muted colours and tones, echoing the classic Safari colours, were employed throughout.

Top: Fox Browne Creative were appointed as interior designers and out went the dated African furnishings, and in came a wonderfully contemporary look. The sleekness of the steel bar is offset with a collection of plush upholstered sofas, rustic wooden cocktail tables and encased lighting fixtures that recall Masai huts.

Above: The redesign had to make the most of Kichwa's timeless views, and the dining room was built with three open sides to take advantage of that.

So as to keep pace with the luxury hotel market we needed to add in more than just safari, so we created an interactive kitchen in the dining room where children can learn to cook. We revamped and enlarged the swimming pool and installed an organic vegetable garden in the courtyard of the main lodge, and a library and Safari shop completed what we hoped would be a magical experience for guests.

Added to this, andBeyond were keen to ensure a light footprint, in keeping with their strong conservation ethos. We therefore designed the space for and installed its very own water bottling plant. This plant reduces the camp's carbon footprint and eliminates the need to transport mineral water from the Mara. The Kichwa Tembo team now bottles its own purified mineral water in stylish glass bottles, thereby reducing waste and recycling the bottles.

Also installed were 183 square metres of solar panelling, capable of producing up to 9 400 litres of hot water daily, saving 40,000 litres of diesel per annum, translating into a saving of 106 tons of CO_2.

Above and left: The organic gardens were constructed as raised beds surrounding a small pond that doubles as a watering tank, and as long as vegetables the baboons don't like such as black cocktail tomatoes, chillies and kale are planted they don't come near it.

Previous pages: We redecked the swimming pool, Fox Browne Creative sourced contemporary sunloungers to match and the warthogs seemed to approve of their new watering hole.

Below and bottom: At the end of a long day, to return to these wonderful tents now positioned looking out over the Mara, and have the wildlife come to you, is an unbeatable experience. A muted palette of safari colours with an occasional splash of tribal red, gives these rooms a serenity and peace.

Sandibe Safari Lodge
Okavango Delta, Botswana

Architect **Michaelis Boyd with Nick Plewman Architects**
Interior Design **Fox Browne Creative**

THE BRIEF: Almost as soon as we'd finished Kichwa Tembo, the Enthovens approached us again to work on Sandibe. This was to be a sustainable new build safari lodge located on a UNESCO World Heritage site in northwest Botswana. The brief was to replace the previous lodge building with a dramatic design that would provide a five star experience whilst capturing the tranquillity of the Okavango Delta region - all to a lighter, more sustainable footprint. We were to work once again with architect Nicholas Plewman, and this was a project he cared about very much. This turned out to be one of our favourite projects, as we discovered that without planning permission to worry about we had complete freedom with our design.

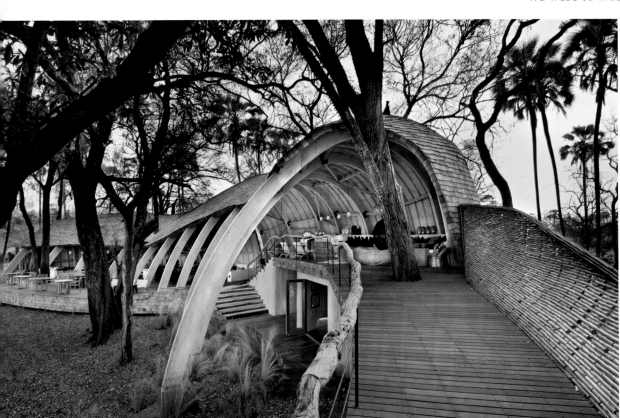

Left: We quickly rejected the notion of a cluster of huts, concentrating instead on one dramatic building with twelve elevated bedrooms. The curved trusses with shingle roofs grounds the building into the landscape.

Above: Inside the main building, Fox Browne Creative interior designed using a soft textural palette with pale timber walls and highlights of copper. This look is both luxurious and utterly in keeping with the trees and colours around it.

Right: Design inspiration came from indigenous weavers' nests and the elusive, nocturnal Pangolin, anteaters covered in tough overlapping scales with an undulating elongated body. The walls were clad with cedar shingles to imitate this quality, and the buildings constructed with curved Glulam South African pine beams and Eucalyptus gum poles sourced from sustainable forests. The buildings were elevated and respectfully built around existing trees.

The new buildings had to be built of bio-degradable materials. Separated from civilisation by a hundred miles of swampland, river crossings and rough tracks, the site had to be completely cleared of all previous non degradable material – literally hundreds of tonnes of demolished bricks and mortar were gently removed from the forest and trucked out of the delta. Seventy percent of the luxury lodge's not insubstantial energy requirements had to be of sustainable origin. Notwithstanding the above our clients expected a boutique hotel that would deliver the very highest standards of luxury to its guests. This meant that in addition to its unique and inspiring design, there could be no compromise on power, the copious hot water supply, luxury bathing and food preparation must equal the best hotels in the world. The sorts of compromises that inform most eco lodges were not acceptable here. Luckily we could respond to this by installing photo voltaic cells that produced the electricity and solar thermal panels and heat exchangers to transfer surplus heat generated by refrigeration units for the hot water.

Curved steps were built up to the main lodge through segments of shingled skin to a raised dining terrace. We created a further flight of steps to a bar and lounge area with a dramatic curved bar and sweeping timber ribs. From here a walkway was built leading to a spectacular ficus tree and viewing platform where guests could enjoy unrivalled views over the Delta. The project was not without its problems. When the curved support beams eventually arrived, each beam had a different radius, meaning we could not fit a single one into place. Without the help of our engineers, De Villiers Sheard, and our contractor Adriaan van der Merwe who worked day and night for a week to replane them, we would have gone over budget and over schedule.

Above and right: Sandibe is built almost entirely of wood. Laminated pine beams give a strong curvelinear shape, and the building is formed like an inverted boat. There are twelve luxury suites, each with its own plunge pool, decorated in warm neutrals and bronzes.

"Good architecture lets nature in." *I.M.Pei*

Far Left: The pangolin inhabits and carries its shelter with it, creating a home however far it travels. This influence can be seen in the private sitting room adjoining each suite, with its curved walls embracing an open log fire, creating a feeling of seclusion and shelter.

Above: A timber platform extends over the swampland, surveying the African landscape.

Arijuju Lodge
Borana Conservancy Estate,
Laikipia, Kenya

Architect **Michaelis Boyd with Nick Plewman Architects**
Interior Design **Life Interior Design**
Landscape Design **Jinny Blom**

THE BRIEF: Our client had fallen in love with and acquired a large piece of land on the Dyer family estate in the foothills of Mount Kenya. We had worked with him before on his London house, and our recent experiences with andBeyond gave us the right credentials to offer our services for this exciting project. The territory was huge, with only one neighbour at Sirai Lodge, 20km away. Our brief was to create, in the middle of this tough, dry wilderness, a protected haven that merged with its surroundings; the outline would not appear until you actually arrived at the gates. The lodge needed to be self-sufficient and its carbon footprint as low as possible. The plan was to rent the house for private holidays when the owner was not there, so furnishings, fixtures and fittings had to be as luxurious as any other five-star safari lodge.

With thoughts of 'haven', 'hidden' and 'self-sufficient' in mind, we looked for inspiration from one of our favourite buildings – Le Thoronet in the Var, Provence – a 12th century Cistercian abbey. Following the rule of St Benedict the Abbey was designed to be an autonomous community, taking care of its own needs. The design of the buildings was a direct expression of this, using the most basic and pure elements; rock, light and water, to create an austere, pure and simple world for the monks. It is one of the most serene and tranquil places we know, and this was what we wanted to create at Arijuju.

Opposite: Rendering of the exterior shows a design using local stone with a flat roof rather than the traditional thatch, so that the site blends in quietly with the surrounding landscape.

Above and left: A view towards the pool, with a glimpse of the flat roof-tops, which was planted with sedum, an innovation for a game reserve. Through the arched 'cloistered' verandas, is an internal courtyard garden, designed by Jinny Blom.

We teamed up again with Nick Plewman and Life Interiors to bring the project to fruition. An important aspect was to ensure that the extraordinary sunrises and sunsets could be seen from all parts of the house, so we designed the windows to match the Cistercian cloisters we'd created. All the materials were locally sourced, and we owe a huge debt to Ben Jackson, the contractor, who designed and made all the metalwork. A bore hole was sunk to provide water for the entire site, a huge array of solar panels ensures electricity twenty-four hours a day.

Above: A first picture of the dining room to show the arched windows and the serenity of the view.

Right: There are three master suites in the main house, and another guest house, enabling at least two families to stay here and enjoy the game drives, safari walks, swimming, tennis, squash and horse riding.

Begin forwarded message:
Date: 18 August 2010 06:13:34 BST
CC: Alex Michaelis alex@michaelisboyd.com
Subject: Collingham

Dear Architect,

I understand you are managing our project whilst Luke is away. I was forwarded your email commenting on our instructions and have to say was intensely irritated/amused by your comment below, referring to our desire not to have polished concrete in the basement. It seems you were compelled to write.

This is a great shame in our opinion, the lower ground rooms facing the rear garden are planned to be more contemporary spaces with polished concrete that moves seamlessly from inside to outside. With a timber floor internally and a different specification outside the original concept would be lost, no?

Did you re-read your email before you sent it? I hope the answer is no, because if on examination you didn't see that this sort of comment is almost a parody of what one might expect from an architect in a comedy show, then someone at your company should pay for you to go on some sort of course.

In one fell swoop you manage to tell your client that he doesn't have any taste. Is that what they teach you at architect's school? "Today we are going to learn some techniques in looking down our noses at our clients because they love it so much!' Fortunately what I learnt at school was to appreciate that taste was subjective, and that no-one is an expert, least of all those who are foolish and arrogant enough to believe they are.

For future reference, the correct response to our simple request for a wooden floor in the basement goes something like this...

Absolutely. I hear you. Whatever you want. Will get some samples of wood for you choose from.

Get the idea. Just to remind you, this is a house which I and my family will be living in, not you.
If you love polished concrete so much, be my guest and cover your own home in it. It is NOT what we want. If we had wanted a polished concrete floor in the basement we would have asked for one. Yes, they were indicated in the original design plans, but, unless no-one has told you, we scrapped those plans some time ago.

I don't want to argue aesthetics here, pointing out that in some circles polished concrete is now looking like the equivalent of the food world's Black Cod with Miso - cutting edge once and fresh once but now seen all over the place - in short, a cliché. I don't want to say that because that is just my opinion and as we have already established in chapter one of this email, opinion on taste or purely subjective.

If I want timber floors in the basement, that's what I will have. If I want my floors covered in muesli with shag pile carpeting on the walls that is what I will have.

Therefore in future I would be grateful if you would keep your patronising comments to yourself. They are not helpful and only drive a wedge between the client and yourselves, which is stupid when you are running a business again there are course you can go on to learn this.

That's it. It's bad luck for you that I am now on holiday and have the time to send these nice long emails. I'll put this incident down to your enthusiasm for your work and an obvious lack of experience. Let's draw a line under this - I assume drawing lines is well within your skill-set.

Not pleasant being patronised is it?

Just off to polish some concrete.

Yours,
Jimmy Mulville

www.hattrick.co.uk <http://www.hattrick.co.uk/>

Date: Wed, 7 Dec 2011 15:16:13
To: alex@michaelisboyd.com<alex@michaelisboyd.com>
Subject: Fwd: Shower Heads

Dear Architect,

We continue to love our new house.Thanks for helping us achieve what we
wanted. If you're around in the week before Christmas we'd like to give
you a festive drink with Luke and Misae. Let me know what works for you
early evening.

Of course there are always a few small things most of which are being
addressed by the admirable Bhuva. However we have a problem with the
shower. Basically we asked for a large rose and are now being told, it
seems, that the power of the water coming through even with the aid of
a pump is not sufficient. Apparently it's all our fault according to the
bathroom guy, whom you know I think, for wanting this large a rose. I'm
thinking that this kind of rose which is made commercially cannot be
unusable. In fact I know it isn't because we had the same rose in our old
place with a strong pressure of water.

We're told by Bhuva that it might be the pipe supplied to feed the rose is
too narrow in diameter.

Oh and the solution to this problem according to the increasingly popular
bathroom guy is, yes, you've guessed it, fit a smaller rose! It's the
bathroom fitter's way of saying, "I told you so". I haven't met him yet but
am really looking forward to it.

You've normally got a smart solution to these kinds of things? What do you
think? Apart from fitting a rose that the bathroom guy wants but we don't.

Best

Jimmy

Jimmy Mulville
Managing Director
Hat Trick Productions

Index